How To Be a Better Boss

LESSONS FROM
ACTUAL BUSINESS OWNERS

Gary Vaughan

Art: Alberts Illustration & Design
Editor: Proof Positive Editing
Formatter: Kate Tilton's Author Services, LLC

DISCLAIMER

WHAT WOULD A GOOD BOOK BE WITHOUT A disclaimer? A book by its very nature goes through many hands. First, it gets edited, then proofed, then laid out. It's a process and not one without some risk of error. While every effort has been taken to ensure that all information contained is completely accurate, some of the information is merely an educated guess. You know the saying: "Reasonable minds may disagree."

You agree to hold Gary Vaughan, and his affiliates, harmless for the information presented or omitted.

I am dedicating this book to my wife, Sharon, who has supported my "this and that" personality for over forty years, and our children, Christy and Kevin, and our grandchildren, Ben, Maggie, and Jacob (JJ). I am blessed and I never take that for granted.

FOREWORD

THIS IS NOT A TYPICAL BUSINESS OWNER "HOW-to" book. This book is a collection of *real life* experiences I have had over the past ten plus years as a consultant working with business owners and managers to help grow their business or to turn around a struggling business. I share these experiences to get you thinking about the opportunities you might be missing in your organization. As a business owner or manager, we learn what "to do" through our experiences and we learn what "not to do" through many of those same experiences. Many of us learn how to run a business from a technical college or university education. Those lessons are valuable, but so are the lessons learned from the proverbial "school of hard knocks" we live through as we run our businesses.

I challenge you to read a couple lessons at a time when you need five minutes away from the day-to-day routine. Share your favorite lessons with your management team to help them see opportunities that your organization might have been missing. Maybe you'll even see yourself in the role of The Boss. So sit down, relax, read, and *think*.

WHO IS GARY VAUGHAN?

GARY VAUGHAN HAS shown a passion for helping business owners through his work as a consultant, where he works with top-tier management to grow shareholders' equity. He launched Guident Business Solutions, LLC, a management and consulting firm, in 2009. He specializes in improving financial results through an increased understanding of financial statements and organizational efficiencies.

Gary has management experience in several industries including retail, petroleum, and manufacturing. He has been a partner in a manufacturing firm where he was responsible for financials, administration, human resources, and safety compliance. Gary has held a profession in human resources certification through SHRM, the Society for Human Resource Management.

Gary has held the position of associate director of an Entrepreneurship Center at Fox Valley Technical

College. He joined Concordia University Wisconsin in 2003, where he taught both undergrad and graduate courses, including MBA courses in Corporate Finance and Strategic Management. In 2009, he joined the faculty of Lawrence University in Appleton, Wisconsin as a lecturer in Innovation and Entrepreneurship.

TABLE OF CONTENTS

Marketing Strategies

BUSINESS MANAGEMENT SKILLS

"THERE IS NOTHING WRONG
WITH CHANGE IF IT IS IN
THE RIGHT DIRECTION."

Winston Churchill
Former British Prime Minister, Army Officer, and Writer

LESSON 1:
EVERY BUSINESS OWNER SHOULD OWN A WHITE SHIRT!

I ONCE HAD A CLIENT who owned an auto repair business. He was a very good mechanic and worked on cars all the time. You could often find several cars and trucks in his backyard waiting to be worked on. As his family grew, his wife wanted the vehicles out of the yard. His solution was to start a business and open a shop 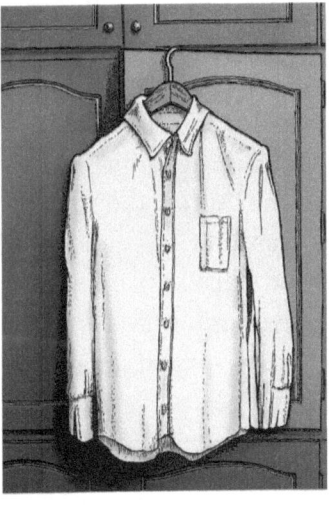 of his own. He called me because his banker was asking him for accurate financial statements.

He would work twelve hours a day under the hood of a car and then spend a half hour every other day trying to get caught up on his book work. I would visit him every week on a specific day, let's say Tuesday, for ninety minutes. During our initial conversations—actually all the time we worked together—he would give me grief that I wore a white shirt. "As you know," he would say, "anyone who wears a white shirt all the time definitely is not working." He would wear the typical blue and gray striped mechanic's shirt covered with grease and dirt stains.

Often times when I first came to work with him, he did nothing but shop work from the time I last left him to the time I arrived the next week. He spent little time on the current financials or planning for the future. I needed to get him engaged in working "on the business" verses always working "in the business". A great book that stresses this concept is *E-Myth Revisited* by Michael Gerber.

So one day I bought him his own white shirt and suggested he wear it when we work together. The white shirt signified the time he was to work on the business. When I arrived he would take off the dirty blue and gray shirt and put on the white shirt for the entire ninety minutes we worked together. After we were done we would hang the white shirt against the back of his office door and put on the blue and gray shirt again. It was obvious to me he was much more comfortable in his blue/gray shirt than the white shirt.

We discussed how making a good business decision on bad financials hardly ever leads to positive results. He began to understand that analyzing his past performance and working on developing a business strategy was as important as working on the engines he loved so much. The white shirt was a symbol of him as "the business owner". He needed to clear his mind and concentrate on what we were doing in his office when we were together. At the end of the day he really was a good business owner and is still in business today.

"ALONE, WE CAN DO SO LITTLE. TOGETHER, WE CAN DO SO MUCH."

Hellen Keller
Former Author, Political Activist, and Lecturer

LESSON 2:
I'M MUCH SMARTER IN A ROOM FULL OF PEOPLE!

As I work with small to mid-size business I struggle to convince the business owner that he or she would be much better off with an advisory team. As business owners we think we are pretty good. We are! That's how we get to be business owners. But that sense of confidence can also be a deterrent to business owners increasing the owner's equity in their organizations.

A client once said to me, "I can't talk to my employees, I can't talk to my spouse, I can't talk to my banker, who can I talk to about my business challenges?" This is a problem in a lot of smaller organizations and the answer is "your advisory board".

For most advisory boards of smaller companies the board members are volunteers. For starters, I recommend inviting your banker, your lawyer, your CPA, and an old sage (retired) business professional you know, maybe from your church or Rotary Club, etc. In my experience an odd number of members is best for voting and I would keep it small to start, seven members at most. These people may not know your business as intimately as you do, but they do know business!

You can meet once a month or once a quarter depending on your preference and the availability of your advisory board members. I have had advisory boards for most of my businesses and I have found them to be invaluable. I know they have saved me money and/or helped me make more money for my companies. In turn, I have served on advisory boards for universities, chamber of commerces, non-profit businesses, and for-profit businesses. In both cases, either having an advisory board or serving on an advisory board, I can honestly say that I benefited as much as the organizations did and I have some very close relationships as a result.

Take a close look at including an advisory board in your business strategy. A collective brain trust with diverse experiences can help you to establish best practices and help you avoid re-inventing the wheel. Throughout my career, "I have always been smarter in a room full of *smart* people than I have been by myself!" I'm betting you will be smarter too.

"THE SINGLE
BIGGEST PROBLEM IN
COMMUNICATION IS
THE ILLUSION THAT IT
HAS TAKEN PLACE."

George Bernard Shaw
Former Playwright, Critic, and Political Activist

LESSON 3:
I THOUGHT I WAS A GOOD COMMUNICATOR—NOT SO MUCH!

At one time in my career I was a partner in a manufacturing company with a multi-million dollar annual budget. I pride myself on being a good communicator and I was—at work. I remember one particular month when we experienced a $20,000 operating loss. I was frustrated with our poor performance and called all managers into an executive meeting to assess the root cause of the problem and to develop a strategy to correct the operations so we would not have to experience this type of loss again. I was satisfied we had the problem identified and a good plan of action going forward. Nonetheless, I was still very frustrated with our poor performance.

Later in the day when I arrived home, my wife was at the kitchen counter preparing our meal for the night. She sensed that I was frustrated and asked what was wrong. I said, "We had a terrible month and lost $20,000." I immediately went outside to "shoot some buckets" in our driveway. This was one of the ways I de-stressed at the end of the day. After a while I was feeling much better and went inside for dinner.

I noticed my wife was very stressed and I then asked her what was wrong. As you can imagine, the whole while I was outside de-stressing with the basketball, she was in the kitchen fretting that we were in dire straits and on the road to losing our house and all we'd worked for. I realized I gave her half of the information she needed, and the worse half at that. I promptly explained that our team of bright managers had already met and developed a fix for the problem.

I also realized that to my wife who managed our home budget, a $20,000 loss was a huge number that from her viewpoint could cause a bankruptcy of the company. Don't get me wrong, it's a lot of money in any organization, but as part of a multi-million dollar operation, it was not going to crash the organization. I then helped her to understand the relationship of the numbers so she would feel more at ease.

For a guy who prides himself on being a very good communicator at work, I realized I fell way short at home. At that point I realized I needed to make a more concerted effort to be as good a communicator at home as I was at work.

"EVEN IF YOU ARE ON THE RIGHT TRACK, YOU'LL GET RUN OVER IF YOU JUST SIT THERE."

Will Rogers
Former American Stage and Film Actor

LESSON 4:

DOES YOUR COMPANY HAVE A SEAT AT THE TABLE?

FOR MANY YEARS I HAVE SEEN OWNERS OF SMALL to mid-size businesses manage their companies like they were one of their children or dependents. Then when things go awry they call people like me for help. My advice to them is to *"corporatize"* their companies.

I often see business owners who think of themselves and their businesses as one entity. These owners act as if the business could not function without them; they feel as if they are the lifeline to the organization. This is almost always not the case. Any company which is to be sustainable must not be dependent on any one individual, no matter how important that position is within the organization.

To demonstrate this I often pull a chair up to the table where we are working and ask the owner to imagine that the business is occupying that chair. As you can imagine they look at me as if I've lost it! I ask them if they can personally fund the next payroll. They usually say, "well no". I tell them that the company can and does. I ask them if they can make rent, make the work-man's compensation payment, make the next interest payment, and so forth. The company can and will do all these things.

As the business owner you must realize that the company has more power than any one individual in the organization. Customers are customers of the company, not of any one salesperson or business owner. Owners must treat their companies with respect and not manage them as if they were a child or dependent.

In other words, business owners must *"corporatize"* the way they see the business. You have to start thinking and acting differently toward your company if you want it to be sustainable. Let the organization grow up and become its own entity, separate from your own persona. As the business owner you will set the culture of the organization, this is true; but also know as the owner you must understand your limitations and the power of the organization. If you don't set a place at the table for your company, you will be the glass ceiling. Next meeting pull up a chair and invite the company into the conversation; begin the transition of power from the owner to the organization and watch your people and the company grow.

"ALWAYS PASS ON WHAT YOU HAVE LEARNED."

Master Yoda
STAR WARS

LESSON 5
HAVE YOU EVER WORKED FOR SOMEONE WHO COULD SEE THE FUTURE?

A S YOUNG MANAGERS MOST OF US HAD THE privilege of being mentored by an old sage in our organizations. I remember working with one such person who always seemed to know the future. He seemed to have the power to see around blind corners and know what was coming. I often would ask him, "How did you know that was going to happen?" Mind you this was way before using "The Force" and *Star Wars* was popular!

How does this work? It is the difference between a reactive or proactive leader. A proactive leader will anticipate various scenarios the company or organization may encounter around that blind corner. They are proactively developing contingency plans (strategies) for each of the probable scenarios. They have those various strategies in their "back pockets", at-the-ready to employ when the threat or opportunity presents itself. When the time is right, the proactive leader simply chooses the best solution and takes full advantage of the situation.

To the rank and file employees it looks like the leader knew exactly what was going to happen. This ability to *seemingly* be able to see the future gives the organization confidence in the leader and could save the organization from spending unnecessary resources. This proactive leader sets aside time to work "on their business" creating strategies and developing a leadership style that often allows an organization to take advantage of opportunities before their competition can react.

As the great leader Yoda once said, "Do or do not, there is no try!" Seeing the future is possible, even without "The Force", if you "Do" decide to be that proactive leader.

"LOOK FIRST INSIDE
YOUR ORGANIZATION
FOR SOLUTIONS, YOUR
EMPLOYEES WILL
OFTEN HAVE THE
ANSWERS YOU SEEK."

Gary Vaughan,
Educator, Author, Speaker, and Entrepreneur

LESSON 6:
STANDARD OPERATING PROCEDURES (SOPS): WELL WORTH IT!

ONE OF MY CLIENTS WANTED TO KNOW HOW to increase profits without raising prices. I asked if they had established standard operating procedures (SOPs) in the various departments. The boss said that would be impossible and way too costly and time consuming. I then asked if they had *any* SOPs. The answer was no. The boss said if one of his managers wanted to set up SOPs with me that would be fine as long as it didn't take away from his productivity. I found this statement to be curious as SOPs more often than not will enhance productivity and efficiencies. The service manager volunteered to work with me, as his department was always lagging behind the other departments, which were granted more resources.

Our first job was to observe the current procedures and then talk with the crew members asking how we could improve their processes. During one morning break I showed up with a Starbucks cardboard coffee carafe and a dozen donuts and we began to talk. In the fifteen minutes we had during their break period we came up with many procedures that, when implemented, had the potential to improve efficiencies. The manager and I took notes and the next day we came back with the first draft of our SOPs. The crew members liked the fact that we listened to them and had included many of their ideas. Their buy-in was easy after that! They had ownership in the process.

Within a few weeks the crews were beating their estimated times and the quality improved. The boss asked the service manager what was going on and what we had done to make these changes. Needless to say soon afterward I was helping the other managers establish their own SOPs. Of course we were asking the other department employees for their input and suggestions on how we could improve their processes. One of the best features of these improvements was increased quality throughout the company. Especially because this company did not have a dedicated quality control person in the main warehouse, and each department or crew was to be the company's quality control agents.

The company was more profitable by virtue of the increased efficiencies, and the boss understood that many of the answers he was looking for were found by talking with his employees. If I could impart one lesson to the business owners I have worked with over the years it would be, "Look inside your organization for the answers to your questions and the solutions to your challenges." That is where I find most of my answers when I begin to work with a company. Standard operating procedures can and most times will relate to greater profits. They are worth the investment on the front end.

"AN EXPERT IS A MAN
WHO HAS MADE ALL THE
MISTAKES WHICH CAN BE
MADE, IN A NARROW FIELD."

Niels Bohr
Former Physicist and Philosopher

LESSON 7:
YOU ARE THE SUBJECT MATTER EXPERT—PROMOTE YOURSELF!

ONE YEAR MY WIFE AND I WERE TOYING WITH selling our home, which we lived in for twenty years. She is a farm girl with a horticulture degree. Needless to say our backyard looks awesome in the summertime, so I said if we do sell we would have to sell in the summer months because I could get an additional $10,000 for the house just because of the plantings. I'm one who has learned to really appreciate the different colors and how the plantings add to our home's ambience, but I in no way would have the vision to create it myself. My wife is the subject matter expert in our family when it comes to plants.

Most business owners are subject matter experts in their fields. More often than not, I work with business owners who have great technical ability but need help developing the management skills to achieve their goals in a fast-growing business. I like to suggest that they volunteer on the radio or speak at chamber events promoting themselves as subject matter experts in their chosen fields. Many of these types of organizations are looking for speakers and do not have a huge budget to pay the national or even regional speakers to come speak at events. From my experience many of the local business experts I hear speak at events are more in tune with the culture of the area and the challenges faced by many in the audience.

Volunteering to be on an expert panel can get you and your business free advertising and help your promotional budget get more bang for the buck. If you think about it, wouldn't your customers rather have work done from an organization that is owned by a subject matter expert?

I come from a Midwest state and many of the business owners I work with find it hard to self-promote. These professionals are often uncomfortable in front of crowds or in a crowded room. This also affects their ability to network and "work a room" during professional events and conferences. For many, networking is a learned skill. This is why speaking about a subject that you know inside and out is the first step to better networking for your business.

Promote yourself as that subject matter expert in your area or region; it has the potential to increase profits and open doors for you and your business that you might not even know exist.

"NO MAN WILL MAKE
A GREAT LEADER WHO
WANTS TO DO IT ALL
HIMSELF, OR TO GET THE
CREDIT FOR DOING IT."

Andrew Carnegie
Former Industrialis and Philanthropist

LESSON 8:
HOW DID THE BOSS ACT WHEN THE "TOY" WAS BROKEN?

THERE ARE TIMES WHEN I FIRST ENGAGE WITH a business that I realize the business model that has worked for many years is broken for whatever reason, and my goal is to work with the boss to fix their long-standing business model.

As I begin to work with the boss to assess the challenges of the organization, I often find myself working closely with the key employees of the organization. As we begin our work together it becomes apparent what needs to be improved and what is working well. Often, I come to this assessment through the insight of the key employees. In short, the answers to the problems the business is experiencing are often offered up to me by these seasoned employees.

Why, then, does the boss not know how to fix the problems?

Once the business model is broken and the boss cannot fix it himself or herself, they may become frustrated because they feel they should have all the answers—it's their business after all. The real answer lies in poor communication; the boss has not engaged these key employees, who are the subject matter experts, to help solve the issues. Every so often I see the boss disengaging because their "toy" is now broken, and doing business is frustrating and not as fun as it used to be. In effect, the boss has a broken toy caused by playing too rough with it and mismanaging their business.

By working with key employees, we set out to improve the business model and fix the toy. This doesn't happen overnight, and while we are in the process of establishing a viable business model, the boss remains frustrated and disengaged. Once the business begins to show improvements, reestablish a positive bottom line, and is running smooth again, I often see the boss want to reengage and run the company again. The boss sees that the toy is fixed and is fun to play with again. This may help the boss feel good again, but it is very frustrating to the company's key employees, who are the real reason for the business's recovery.

As the boss, you must stay engaged with the business and be a part of the solution, not exiting when the business is underperforming and reengaging when the cash is flowing. Most business owners would say, "No business owner would do this!", but I can assure you I have seen it time and time again. Don't get caught up in this trap, stay engaged when the toy is broken and be part of the solution. Engage your key employees and work together to fix the toy!

"ONE CANNOT TRAIN SOMEONE TO BE PASSIONATE - IT'S EITHER IN THEIR DNA OR IT'S NOT."

Richard Branson
Business Magnate, Investor, Author, and Philanthropist

LESSON 9:
SO YOU WANT TO START A BUSINESS? THROW OUT THE JOKERS!

WHEN I WAS A CHILD MY SISTERS AND I LIKED to play a card game called Rummy 500. Those of you who know this game understand the goal is to reach 500 points before anyone else. In rummy all cards are counted as their face value except the jokers. They were considered wild cards and we could choose their value to make them equal to any card in the deck.

When I was in college, my buddies and I liked to play poker. When I played with them we were serious and played for money. Because we were playing for money, we didn't have wild cards and we didn't use the jokers.

I often advise people who are considering starting a new business to throw out the jokers, eliminating them from the deck. When starting a new business the jokers are not wild cards but instead "failure cards". The thought of failure is not an option when starting a new business. You cannot even have the failure card in the deck because when the going gets tough—and it will—you don't want to be tempted to throw that failure card onto the table.

So often when I see businesses that have failed in the first year or two, I see a business owner who held that failure card in their hand and eventually played it when cash flow was tight, or worse, nonexistent. Don't let this happen to you. Take the failure card out of your deck before you start your new business and do not consider failure as an option. What this does is forces the business owner to find innovative ways to make the business work. A resource I suggest if you are considering starting a new business is *The Lean Startup* by Eric Ries. When money is involved, there should be no jokers in the deck. Failure is not an option!

"WE CANNOT SOLVE THE
PROBLEMS WITH THE SAME
THINKING WE USED WHEN
WE CREATED THEM."

Albert Einstein,
Theoretical Physicist, Developed Theory of Relativity

LESSON 10:

RELEASE THAT STRANGLEHOLD YOU HAVE ON YOUR COMPANY.

M OST OFTEN WHEN I AM CONTRACTED TO come into a business, it is because the boss has asked me to help solve a problem that has them stumped. During one of my first conversations with the boss, I usually state that the solutions are often found within the organization. I am most often told, "Not in my business. I have looked everywhere for the cause of the problem and I can't find it." It has been my experience that it doesn't take long for someone from outside the organization with a fresh set of eyes to identify the issue(s).

In a recent client call, I had to confront the boss and say, "That stranglehold you have around the throat of your business is the issue!" The boss looked at me with a bewildered expression and said, "What the heck are you talking about?" I am talking about the stranglehold the boss has on the talent in the business, the smart knowledgeable people who know the issues and know some of the solutions but are not able to act because the boss wants to control everything. The boss has a stranglehold, a death grip around the throat of the business's efficiencies, talent, innovation, and growth.

The personality of the boss trickles down throughout the whole organization. If the boss rules with a death grip, it gives the management team free rein to rule with their own death grips, and before you know it you and your management team have suffocated the organization, stifling productivity and growth. If you are one of these bosses or are working for a boss like this, you can identify with this image.

The solution to the organization's problems? Loosen your death grip on the business and start to control the business as if you were using a Ouija board. Remember the board game you might have played as a child? You lightly touched the planchette and magical things began to happen. Well, I am suggesting that magical things can begin to happen in your business as you start to loosen your stranglehold on the business and begin to control your business with a much lighter touch and let your talented, knowledgeable team help you solve the problems.

Reestablish a culture of cooperation and teamwork. This can be a bit awkward at first, but your organization will welcome the new direction with open arms, especially when they see the boss has already identified the issue and has bought a Ouija board to practice with. Only half joking!

Problems will always surface within a business, that is for certain. How you handle them and how you search out the solutions within your organization is the real trick. If the boss encourages their team to become pro-active and identify potential issues, allowing employees the autonomy to eliminate the root causes of the potential problems before they become problems, the boss won't need trickery. I might even suggest going out and buying a Ouija board to frame and hang in your office, just as a reminder—not joking!

"THE FIRST STEP IN
GROWING YOUR BUSINESS
IS TO "CORPORATIZE"
YOUR WAY OF THINKING."

Gary Vaughan,
Educator, Author, Speaker, and Entrepreneur

LESSON 11:
STEP #1 – YOU ARE A BUSINESS FIRST!

WHEN I FIRST BEGIN WORKING WITH A NEW business, I often hear business owners say they are printers, landscapers, mechanics, etc. The first step in changing a culture and growing a business is to change the way the business owner sees their company. You are a business owner who is first running a business that happens to do printing, you are a business owner who is first running a business that happens to do landscaping, and you are a business owner who is first running a business that happens to repair automobiles. It's a new discipline for most small to mid-size business owners who relate the business to their personal talents.

One of the businesses I was a partner in was a sign company. We built the types of signs you see on the street corners and on the fronts of buildings. We had a talented workforce, but the business was stagnant. In order for us to grow the business we had to change the way we thought of ourselves. Most all of our employees saw our business as a sign company building signs. The business had the ability to be much more than a sign company, but first we had to change our culture. As owners we had to begin to think of ourselves as a business that just happened to build signs. Even more, we had to think of ourselves as first running a business that had the ability to manufacture things other than just signs.

Once we began to shift our thinking in this direction, we started to see all the potential the business had to offer. Our sales staff began to look for opportunities in our market to partner with area manufacturing companies who had overflow work. We had capacity in our workforce and in our facility to take on their overflow. As a result, we began to manufacture items for other companies, creating revenue streams that didn't exist before and that added profits to our bottom line. By the time I left eight years later, our business had grown top-line sales by 800% and had customers throughout the United States and Canada.

The challenge is "business verses company" thinking. When a business owner opens their mind and creates a culture that sees the company as business first, the opportunities will show themselves. We discovered that we were first and foremost a business that just happened to be in manufacturing.

"GOOD LEADERSHIP CONSISTS OF SHOWING AVERAGE PEOPLE HOW TO DO THE WORK OF SUPERIOR PEOPLE."

John. D. Rockefeller,
American Industrialist

LESSON 12:
THE BOSS NEEDS TO BE THE COACH FOR THE TEAM.

I BEGAN WORKING WITH A COMPANY WHERE THE boss was frustrated and exhausted. The boss was playing the roles of operations manager, sales manager, and being the boss over the entire company. The boss had begun the company many years ago and the revenues had grown into the millions of dollars. Now the boss felt like he had a "tiger by the tail" and was just hanging on without really controlling anything.

I asked the boss why he felt he needed to fill the management roles for all the departments, and he stated none of his employees were ready to take on the responsibilities. The boss was a big sports fan, so I used a sports analogy to explain what I was seeing.

The boss had several key positions open on his team and was waiting for an MVP player to show up to occupy those positions. Because the boss felt he did not have an MVP player on his team, he left the positions vacant or tried to fill them himself. Imagine if he was coaching a football team and the right tackle position on the offensive line was left vacant and the quarterback was left to fend for himself. As a coach, we would never do this. We would fill the position with the best player we had, knowing that the player was not MVP quality, but that having a person in the position was better than leaving the position vacant. By not filling the operations manager position or the sales manager position, the boss left others on the team vulnerable and unable to do their jobs to the best of their abilities.

The boss needed to fill the two positions with the best players available and then coach those employees into MVP players. By trying to do too many jobs and fill too many positions, the boss didn't have time to coach his players and was frustrating himself and his team members. The results were not what the boss wanted.

If you think about this, it was to be expected that one person could not do the job of three and produce the results the company needed. After I explained this to the boss, he told me one of the underlying reasons for not filling the positions was the boss felt he could not afford the payroll because the departments were not producing the expected profits.

The boss was trying to save the payroll expense and thinking he could do the job of three positions: the operations manager, the sales manager, and being the boss! This is typical because in the early years of the company that is what the boss did—he did everything. But now that the company had grown, one person doing everything was not possible. The boss needed to see the payroll expense as an investment in his employees.

Most companies do not have a roster of all MVP players, so the boss needs to fill each position with the best player possible and then coach them into MVP status! I have learned not to underestimate the abilities of good people; often they will surprise us and do a great job when given the chance.

"MANAGEMENT IS EFFICIENCY IN CLIMBING THE LADDER OF SUCCESS; LEADERSHIP DETERMINES WHETHER THE LADDER IS LEANING AGAINST THE RIGHT WALL."

Steven Covey,
former American Educator, Author, Businessman, and Speaker

LESSON 13:
WHAT THE BOSS STRESSES, THE EMPLOYEES ACCOMPLISH. MAKE IT THE RIGHT MESSAGE!

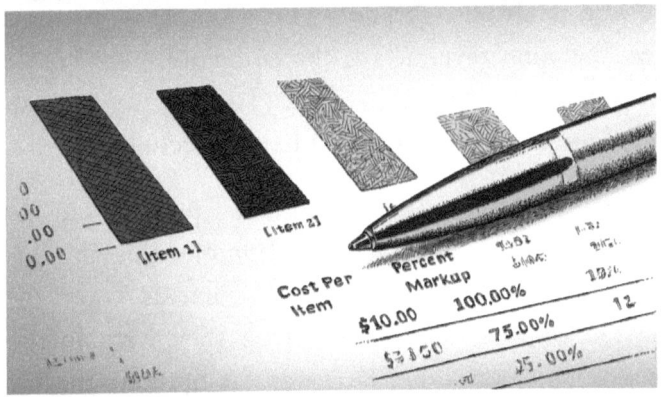

WHEN I FIRST BEGIN WORKING WITH A COM-
pany I sit in on the managers meeting and just listen. What I often find is that the staff is focused on what the boss stresses as important. They instruct their direct reports to accomplish the goals set forth by the boss in these department meetings. The problem I sometimes see is that the boss is sending the wrong message or a partial message.

For example, in one meeting during a review of the prior month's financials, each department head reported to the boss what their actual revenues were compared to the annual budgeted numbers. Then the boss asked what the budgeted revenue goals were for the next month and how each department manager was going to achieve those revenue goals.

Afterward, the boss expressed frustration to me about the lack of gross profit from each department as it pertained to the annual budget goal. During our discussion I asked if the departments were hitting their revenue goals and the boss said, "Yes, as a matter of fact, the total revenue for the company was ahead of last year and ahead of budget." I said I was not surprised as that is what I would have expected.

The boss asked me to explain, and I pointed out that the department heads were focusing on achieving their department's revenues goals and that is what they stressed to their staff. The reason they were focused on revenues is because that was the message the boss was constantly stressing. I suggested the boss also stress gross profit goals along with revenue goals in the next department meeting.

The next meeting the boss asked about the actual revenues and gross profits compared to the budgeted revenues and gross profit goals, and as you can imagine the department heads were not prepared to discuss the gross profits of their departments. It did not take long before the department heads were required to report on both actual revenues and gross profits compared to the budgeted revenues and gross profit goals at their managers meetings.

As the department heads stressed revenues and gross profits, their staff began to find ways to save small incremental dollars, and soon the company began to show measurable gains on profitability without raising prices. The worst thing the boss could have done was to discipline or replace a department manager due to underachieving their gross profit goals when they *were* achieving what the boss was stressing: their top-line revenue goals.

Employees do not get up in the morning and come to work to screw up. They want to do their best for the company, and when the boss sets the proper goals, often the employees will work very hard to accomplish those goals. If the financial results are below expectation, look first at the message. Send the right message to your team and they will do their best to respond with the desired results.

"HE IS STRONG WITH
THE FORCE, BUT TALENT
WITHOUT TRAINING
IS NOTHING."

Jedi Master Luke Skywalker,
Star Wars

LESSON 14:
DON'T UNDERESTIMATE WHAT YOUR EMPLOYEES DON'T KNOW.

WHILE EVALUATING A NEW CLIENT, I PARTICIpated in their management meeting where the boss and the department managers were reviewing their financial performance from the past month. They were evaluating the financials by department, going over the expenditures line by line. I began to ask questions about the sources of the expenses. I received some very vague answers in some cases and in others I was told, "I have no idea."

I observed that the department managers didn't know what success looked like. They didn't have a year-over-year comparison to benchmark their performance, nor did they have an annual operating budget to use as a goal for the month, quarter, and year. I asked the boss if he set goals for his managers. He said he shouldn't have to, they are the managers and they should know what they must do to be profitable. "That's what I pay them for" was one of his responses. I said I understood his position and I often run across business owners who have this same viewpoint. But this approach by the boss will not create the results in the owner's equity that he desires.

After interviewing each of the department managers, I gained some more insight on what was one root cause of the problem. Each manager echoed the same message: they were profitable, and they thought they were doing well. In their opinion, since the boss seldom gave them guidance as to what success looked like for each of their departments, they assumed success was simply showing a profit. The boss figured each department manager should know their jobs and understand how to achieve the most profit possible for their respective departments.

In this case the boss truly underestimated what his department managers didn't know. They had no idea what the boss considered as success for their departments, so there was a huge gap between the department managers and the boss in this area.

We set out to define success in each department and, with the department managers' participation, we developed an annual operating budget, identified each department as a profit center, then input the results into their accounting software, and eventually began to analyze the financial performance of each department (profit center). Each month the department managers would ask the accounting department about any irregular expenses they did not understand, and they came to the monthly managers meeting with solutions in hand to correct any issues so the problem did not continue for another month. The boss was very happy with the results and the department managers had defined goals and financials that let everyone know what success looked like. This allowed the company to celebrate their wins!

The boss must stay fully engaged, defining what success looks like and holding employees accountable for their actions. The boss must not underestimate what the employees don't know, for when he or she does this, most often nothing but bad happens. Plan for success and your owner's equity will improve.

"EVERY DAY THAT WE
SPEND NOT IMPROVING
OUR PRODUCTS WAS
A WASTED DAY."

Joel Spolsky,
Co-Founder of Stack Overflow

LESSON 15:
THINK OF YOUR BUSINESS AS A SPIDERWEB.

ARE YOU CONSIDERING WRITING A STRATEGIC plan for your business? When you do, think of your strategic plan using a spiderweb model. Begin with these key areas in mind: management, production, marketing, human resources, finance, sales, and purchasing. Each of these seven areas acts as an anchor point of the spiderweb. When one of these areas is doing poorly the others are affected, like pinging one side of a spiderweb and watching the opposite side vibrate.

To demonstrate I explain when sales are low, financials in the form of cash flow are affected. When HR has to lower the staff count due to cash flow issues, production is affected. When purchasing is out of sync with the rest of the company, then production and financials can be affected. You get the picture.

If this seems familiar and is happening to your organization, changes are in order. Begin your process by evaluating each of these seven areas to determine which area is strong and which area is a weak link within your business. Most often the financials are a weak link and your first target for change. I cannot emphasize enough the importance of having a person on staff that has a strong understanding of how the P/L, cash flow, and balance sheet work together in your organization. Once you are able to validate the accuracy of your financials you can then evaluate your entire organization and begin to create a strategy for greater profits.

Another area that is often neglected and a weak link is purchasing. Think about the amount of dollars your company spends on materials and supplies annually. Most often it runs into the millions of dollars with no one person accountable for the purchases or the inventory. This is an area where a business can recuperate profits without affecting customers or raising prices.

With changes underway in these two areas you can look into a third area: production. Establishing SOPs for your production process will begin to curb waste and improve quality. Quality control begins in the production process. Without established SOPs you will often see employees doing what they feel is best but often not in unison with others in their department or in the organization. We call this Individual Operating Procedures (IOPs). IOPs cause poor quality, poor communications, and lost profits. Here is another area where you can recuperate profits without affecting customers or raising prices.

Other areas to review are sales and marketing. It is important not to begin with these areas because without a profitable business model, by increasing sales you will just cause yourself to work harder for fewer profits. Of course none of these positive changes happen without management driving them. As Jack Welch stated, "Good business leaders create a vision, articulate the vision, passionately own the vision, and relentlessly drive it to completion." Change begins at the top of the organization and is driven throughout the organization by management.

Think of your organization as a spiderweb and understand how the entire organization is affected when you initiate change in any one area, like pinging one side of a spiderweb and watching the opposite side vibrate. Your organization is intricately connected, and your strategic plan should reflect the relationships between these key areas, with your mission statement located in the center of the web, holding it all together.

"THE PEOPLE WHO
ARE CRAZY ENOUGH
TO THINK THEY CAN
CHANGE THE WORLD ARE
THE ONES WHO DO."

Steve Jobs,
*former American Entrepreneur, Industrial
Designer, and Business Magnate*

LESSON 16:
AS BUSINESS OWNERS, WE ARE GAMBLERS!

IT'S TRUE: AS BUSINESS OWNERS, WE ARE GAM-blers. We are willing to take those mitigated risks that our employees are not willing to take. We are willing to bet our savings and oftentimes our homes on a new second location, an expanded master franchise agreement, or new capital that allows us to enter a new market. Whatever the reason for the risk, we are the ones who say, "Yes, I got this!"

Those risks don't always pay off, and sometimes it can cripple you and your company. That is when we need help. But when do we as risk takers feel we can no longer beat the odds and ask for help? Often it is when the pain we feel is extremely high, and the initial risk has developed into a full-grown problem.

As the boss, you have grown to become pain tolerant. The normal day-to-day issues cause you slight pain as you struggle to make payroll or look for funds to fix that old piece of equipment again. The bigger pain points are the larger capital investments you chose to make.

It is as if you look over the cliff and say to yourself, "That doesn't look that bad and I believe I can make this happen." Then you jump off the cliff and for a while there is no pain. You are falling and continue to pick up speed, but so far you feel pretty good about your decisions. Then the first round of financials come through and you realize that second location was not cash flowing, the master franchise agreement caused you to expand too fast, or that new market has tougher competition from hometown businesses. Now you begin to second-guess yourself and think you should not have jumped. You realized this a little late, but better to realize it sooner than later.

But as risk takers and gamblers we still believe we can make it work, so we double down on our bet and invest more dollars into the problem. We begin to feel anxious about the outcome as we continue to pick up speed and the ground is closing in fast. We realize that if nothing changes, only bad is going to happen. Now we decide to reach out for help as a last resort. Hopefully it is not too late.

How can we avoid these types of situations? We know that the real pain does not happen until we hit the ground, so we do not react until that fact is obvious. Why? Because we are eternal optimists! We believe in our abilities to solve problems and make good on our bets. That's the gambler in all business owners.

Reach out earlier, in fact reach out before you jump! Ask for advice from people outside of your organization who have experiences that complement your own. You have the ultimate say, you have the final decision because you own the risk. Make the best decision you can for you and your organization. Don't wait until you realize that nothing but bad is going to happen— often there are not enough resources left to work with to solve our problems if we wait too long to ask for help. As the boss you will always be that gambler—just be aware of the high stakes some of these bets carry and reach out for intel early and often.

"SUCCESS IS JUDGED NOT BY THE POSITION YOU REACH IN LIFE BUT BY THE OBSTACLES YOU HAVE OVERCOME."

Sandeep Jauhar,
Cardiologist and Contributing Writer for the New York Times

LESSON 17:
DO YOU KNOW WHEN TO YELL UNCLE?
IT'S GOOD BUSINESS.

A FRUSTRATION OF MINE AND MANY OF THE business owners I work with is understanding when to yell uncle. In other words, when to ask for help. I often get calls from the boss explaining a situation they have gotten themselves into and asking what I can do to help them cope. Most often these calls come when the boss is experiencing cash flow problems and their stress level is high. With hindsight being 20/20, the boss realizes their error and wants help strategizing to minimize the fallout.

One such call was in a company where cash was tight, but the boss got wind of a deal on a piece of equipment and went ahead and purchased it without talking to the finance department. Now to make things worse, the equipment could not be used for several months as it was a seasonal business. The finance staff had to find the funds to purchase the equipment and keep the day-to-day cash flow flowing! As you would expect, this caused strife between the boss and the frustrated finance staff.

This is when I got the call to help relieve the tension. The root cause was a communication issue, especially when the finance department learned of the new equipment purchase after it was completed and then was left to make do. Some may even say it was a respect issue between the boss and the finance staff!

Another example is a call I received from a boss who was very worried about production. Again, cash flow was tight, and to save payroll the boss laid off a few people, one being the highest paid employee on the production floor. Unfortunately for the boss, when his competition found out a quality employee had been laid off, they made an offer, and now that employee was working for the competition. This person had been trained in several jobs and sent to CNC training by the manufacturer of the equipment. This employee was a highly paid person because of his skill set, and I am sure the competition was thrilled to get him.

As business picked up, production would be delayed or at the very least slowed down as the remaining employees did not have the necessary skill set to step into the position—a new employee would have to be hired. Not much we could do after the fact, but I stressed to the boss to call *before* these types of decisions are made, not afterward. Not that I have all the answers, but one thing I do not have are the stress and/or emotions tied to the decisions.

Stress can cloud the facts and often cause the boss to make short-sighted decisions that go against the over-arching strategy of the organization. Losing one very good operator can derail a strategy and set it back months until another high-quality individual is hired and assimilates into the company. Not to mention this person may cost you more payroll than the original employee.

As the boss you must realize when you are under stress and when you need to ask for help outside of your organization. The final decision will always be yours as the boss, the one holding the risk/reward card for the company, but knowing there is a better way to make these types of decisions and knowing when to yell uncle and ask for help is the sign of an experienced business owner.

"PRICE IS WHAT YOU PAY.
VALUE IS WHAT YOU GET."

Warren Buffett,
Chairman and CEO of Berkshire Hathaway

LESSON 18:
BARTERING: I'M NOT A FAN!

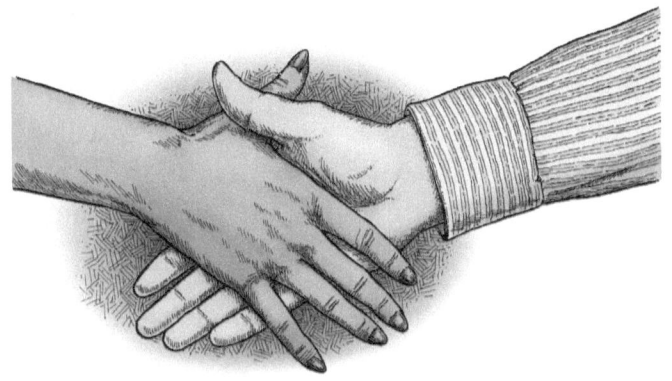

I WAS APPROACHED BY ONE OF MY COMPETITORS who thought I would be interested in buying his business. Anyone who has ever had this happen knows that a business owner just doesn't want to sell their business—something is not working well, and they want out. They may not have a relative or business partner to buy their company, so they go soliciting potential buyers so they can exit the company. They are looking for a succession plan!

I agreed to do a walk-through of his company. If you asked my wife, she would not have been surprised, as she often pointed out with me it was not "either this or that"; most likely I would see things as "this *and* that", and away we go!

As I asked questions and walked through his company, I noticed his breakroom floor. It had a very nice-looking new ceramic tile floor. Now anyone who has ever worked in a manufacturing company would tell you that having a ceramic floor in the breakroom was an anomaly. So I had to ask—why?

The owner said that he did a job for a tile company, and the tile company wanted to barter to pay their bill with a new ceramic floor in his breakroom. The owner stated that it didn't cost him anything to have it installed as the tile company discounted the installation fee so the floor would cost the same amount as the tile company's invoice. Everyone was square, right?

I hope that you have recognized this is not good business.

I decided to go further with this project, so the owner and I signed an NDA form (non-disclosure agreement). This is a legal document that restricted me, the potential buyer, from disclosing the financial information of his company. What I found when I did the financial analysis was his company had a very serious cash flow problem. This was one of the main reasons he was interested in selling his business. This did not surprise me with all the bartering this owner did in his business. He thought he was saving money, but it was a huge liability to the business cash flow.

Imagine you barter for a new ceramic floor (which you do not need) in your breakroom rather than collecting cash for your accounts receivable. Now later in the month your utility company sends you an invoice for the electricity you used for the month. The utility company does not want ceramic tiles as payment for that invoice, they want cash, but what you have are new ceramic tiles, no cash.

I would imagine the tile company could have gotten those tiles for free as a demo, or they may have been a discontinued item that the tile company received credit for and was to destroy. Instead the tile company bartered them for services and saved their cash for other things, leaving the business owner I was talking with in a cash crunch.

Interestingly enough, we did initially come to an agreement and I purchased his company. In that process, when I went to reconcile his balance sheet and validate the barters he was still owed for work he had completed for other companies, many of the other companies had a different amount on their books, and of course the amounts were lower than the balance sheet I was looking at. This confirms that old adage "garbage in and garbage out." If you must, barter with extreme caution, but more importantly, stick with GAAP principles and you won't go wrong.

"GROW WITH DISCIPLINE. BALANCE INTUITION WITH RIGOR. INNOVATE AROUND THE CORE. DON'T EMBRACE THE STATUS QUO."

Howard Schultz,
CEO and Chairman of Starbucks

LESSON 19:
DOES YOUR COMPANY HAVE A SOLID FOUNDATION?

I HAVE THE PRIVILEGE OF HELPING MANY BUSI-ness owners set up their management teams. A company's management team is the foundation from which the boss builds the business. I have found that three positions are essential for success in an organization: a good controller, an excellent operations manager, and a good sales manager. I like to describe these three positions as the legs that hold up the company, as depicted in this drawing.

Imagine your company as this stool. If the legs are weak and wobbly, your company is in danger of collapsing. Let's look at each of these key positions and their order of importance. In most of the organizations I work with, the boss is experiencing stress and anxiety over various cash flow issues. I see cash flow issues as "referred pain"—there is a pain in your wallet, but it is coming from somewhere else in your organization. Most of the time the root cause of cash flow problems are a combination of inconsistent sales, overstock inventories, or just plain poor money management by the boss. How do you fix this? Let's look at each issue separately.

Inconsistent sales can result from the boss trying to run the company and generate the majority of the sales. A good salesperson whose sole responsibility is to drive top-line sales should not spend the majority of their time in the office but out in the market creating relationships and generating orders to feed the machine. The boss cannot do this and run the company on a day-to-day basis with any kind of efficiency. The boss may think he or she can, but if they talk with their key staff they will realize it's not working as well as they think it is.

Hiring a good salesperson and motivating them with a fair commission on sales can free the boss for more "value added" responsibilities such as reconnecting with existing customers and strengthening those important vendor relationships, ultimately improving cash flow without raising prices.

Having a good production manager can also improve cash flow by having a person responsible for the costs associated with the operations of the business. As the boss, think of the amount of money you spend annually on materials and direct labor costs in your organization. When you spend that amount of money, doesn't it make sense to have one person accountable to you for those dollars? The production manager can oversee purchasing and scheduling of the jobs. They can oversee the job costing function after the job is completed to be sure the estimating process is still valid. Today, this job is either not done at all or done by the boss, usually when time allows.

If you are the boss, ask yourself how efficient you are with any of your many jobs, and be honest in your assessment. If you want to validate your answer, ask any one of your key people and tell them to be brutally honest in their answer. Most of the problems in an organization regarding cash flow are apparent to the key employees and they also have a good start on what are the solutions. They just need to be asked their opinion and to work in a culture where they feel safe to answer honestly.

I left the most important position for last: the controller. I am deliberate with naming this position "controller." I am also an advocate for this position to be one of the highest paid positions in your company. Think about why you decided to go into business and what risks you take as a business owner. You should be in business to make a profit and increase your company's owner's equity. You understand the risks of owning your own business and accept them.

I expect that most business owners got into business because they are great technicians or subject matter experts in their chosen fields. Most business owners I work with have not had as much financial training as they would have liked. This lack of formal financial training is one of the main reasons the boss is so anxious about cash flow, and with all their other responsibilities, it's one reason for poor money management in some cases.

My advice to you is to invest in a very good controller. A controller is someone who is formally trained and understands the three financial statements and how they work together. Let this person manage the checkbook, with your guidance of course, because it is still your money they are working with. Free yourself from the day-to-day stress of managing the money and use your time to create value for the organization. I know this is going to be hard and that you may not want to give up the checkbook. Look at it this way, if one of your people were trying to be the salesperson, the production manager, and control the checkbook, and they weren't really doing an efficient job at any of these responsibilities, what would your solution be?

Shore up the foundation of your business by investing in the key people you need in these three foundational areas, the legs to your company. The opportunity cost of you trying to do three jobs is too high, and poor cash flow is the signal that a change is needed. Look inside your company for the signs that something needs to be changed, ask your key employees for their honest opinions, and don't be shy to look outside your organization for solutions. Shore up that foundation and build your dream!

"IN THE LONG RUN, IT'S NOT JUST HOW MUCH MONEY YOU MAKE THAT WILL DETERMINE YOUR FUTURE PROSPERITY. IT'S HOW MUCH OF THAT MONEY YOU PUT TO WORK BY SAVING IT AND INVESTING IT."

Peter Lynch,
Investor, Fund Manager, and Philanthropist

LESSON 20:
DON'T BE SO FRUGAL TODAY THAT IT COSTS YOU YOUR COMPANY TOMORROW.

I RECEIVED A CALL FROM THE BOSS OF A MID-sized company who wanted to talk with me regarding his cash flow challenges. I was referred by his lender, who noticed that despite the company's good revenues and decent net profit, the boss was always experiencing cash flow issues. I asked to see two years of financials and I did an indirect cash flow evaluation on his business along with calculating my top fourteen ratios I use to evaluate the financial health of an organization.

What I found was the company had good operating profit, which meant the organization was generating a healthy sustainable cash flow. I told this to the boss, who immediately asked me, "If I have such good oper-ating cash flow, why do I not have money?" The answer was in the ratio analysis.

When I calculated the return on total assets (ROA), I found the ratio to be very high, too high for this type of business. I began to ask the boss a few questions regarding his building and equipment. Now, the boss was a very frugal man, in my opinion too frugal for the health of the organization. The boss would try not to invest in day-to-day operating supplies, such as not replacing burned out light bulbs if there was still one good bulb working in the light fixture. The boss was proud of this management style, which, by the way, frustrated his employees to no end, not to mention creating an unsafe working environment in some cases.

Why was the ROA ratio too high? The return on the investments was high because the equipment and building were old and tired. The boss hadn't invested anything of consequence into the building for years, he just pocketed the profits year after year. Now the lack of investment had caught up to the boss and he was being forced to invest in the building as the roof was leaking, the HVAC system was obsolete and often not working, the parking lot was deteriorating and had huge holes in the high traffic areas, and many more issues too numer-ous to mention. All these things were eating away at the company's cash flow. We call this "cash cowing" the company, where the boss just collects the profits and does not reinvest enough into capital expenditures to keep the organization going.

Now the boss had to make some tough decisions regarding the building and his equipment. The repairs were extensive and ultimately more expensive now than if they had been addressed when they were much less serious. The boss's frugal personality was catching up to him, and his cash flow was where it showed in the company financials.

I can understand evaluating cash outlays and making the best financial decisions when investing in your business, but in this case the boss's frugal personality was dominating his business decisions in an unhealthy way. Some ratios that show a high percentage are not always a good sign; in this case the company did not have the financial resources to correct all the problems, and the boss ended up having to sell the building in order to save his company.

Business owners are often described as risk takers. The boss in this company may not be considered a risk taker at first sight, but if we look closer, the boss was taking a huge risk with the future of his company by not spending the money to fix the maintenance issues in a timely manner. Remember, you can have good profit with poor cash flow and go out of business, or you can have poor profit and good cash flow and live to fight another day!

"COMPETITION WHOSE MOTIVE IS MERELY TO COMPETE, TO DRIVE SOME OTHER FELLOW OUT, NEVER CARRIES FAR."

Henry Ford,
Founder of the Ford Motor Company

LESSON 21:
FRIENDLY COMPETITION MAKES FOR GREATER PROFITS!

A S WITH MANY BUSINESS OWNERS, I SERVED ON the state board of the industry my company served. I got to know most of my competitors, some of the suppliers, and a few of our legislators as well. We discussed the industry and our own concerns regarding government changes, the economy, and pressures on the labor force. One of the most valuable parts of this experience was the cooperative relationships we developed between each other.

For example, one day I received a phone call from Bill, the owner of my largest wholesale distributor. Bill asked if I had a certain item in inventory. I answered that I did. He then asked if I would drop it off at my competition an hour north of my location. Bill's warehouse was two hours south of my building, so this trip would have been a three-hour one-way drive for his trucks. He said he would replace the inventory item on my next delivery from him. I said I would and promised we would deliver the item by the end of that day.

When I told my foreman what I wanted his driver to do, he looked at me as if I was collaborating with the enemy! He asked, "Why would you do that?" I explained how creating a good relationship with both the distributor and the competition was a very valuable position to be in and would benefit our company in the long run.

The industry we were operating in did most everything by RFPs (requests for proposals), and any job the competitor had we most likely also had a chance to bid on. If we did not get the job, it must have been because the competition underbid us, making the job unattractive for our company, and in that case, letting our competition have a less profitable job was a good thing. I explained to my managers during a management meeting how this type of decision benefits our business as Bill knows we have his back and, in the future, I would expect Bill would have ours.

In all the years I have been in business I have learned that people do business with people they like. We can do business with most anyone we choose, and as we have a choice, we do business with people we like and trust. These relationships don't happen overnight, but when we achieve this status with other business owners, it benefits the bottom line of our company. Truth be told, Bill and I enjoyed a close business relationship, often talking with each other years after I sold that business.

As the boss, one of your main jobs is to drive profitability for you as the owner, your employees as stakeholders in the business, and your investors as creditors in the venture. I often say, "Back in the 1980s and 1990s and even in the early 2000s, we could make money by accident!" Back then the boss didn't have to be so strategic in his thinking, but today as Thomas Freidman states, "The world is flat!" and we are all operating in a global economy. The boss will need every advantage to succeed.

Getting to know your competition, joining state boards and other industry organizations, and being the boss that others want to do business with can greatly benefit your reputation and increase the bottom line of your company, ultimately improving your owner's equity.

"GOOD HABITS ARE THE KEY TO ALL SUCCESS. BAD HABITS ARE THE UNLOCKED DOOR TO FAILURE."

Og Mandino,
American Author

LESSON 22:
WE ARE CREATURES OF HABIT. MAKE THEM GOOD HABITS!

I HAVE TRIED VERY HARD TO MAKE THESE CHAP-
ters not sound like a parent's voice speaking in your
ear. And I fully understand the boss does not like to be
bossed. With that said, here I go talking about good
habits and bad habits exhibited by the boss, particu-
larly regarding cash management.

In good times and in bad—especially bad—I get
questions regarding cash flow. Since COVID-19 has
appeared, this is especially true as the boss struggles
to meet the company's financial obligations. This chapter focuses on patterns I have observed about which
businesses suffer more than others. As the boss, your

business will take on your vision and most often your personality, including your good and bad habits.

We are creatures of habit. If the boss is frugal and manages his personal finances well, I often find the business is in a good financial position. If the boss has trouble managing his personal finances, such as overspending or living paycheck to paycheck, the business will often have the same challenges. The result is a low cash reserve to draw from in an economic downturn. The situation is not limited to low-earning individuals. Some of my clients are professionals working in medical fields, running their own clinics and making mid-six figure incomes, yet I find some of them live paycheck to paycheck.

This bad habit will migrate into the business's culture, showing up as a cash flow issue. The boss does not come to work, flick a switch and operate as a very good cash manager, then leave work, flick a switch and become a very poor cash manager at home. We are creatures of habit. We do not flick personalities on and off like we do a light switch. Good cash management is an individual personality trait.

When the boss finally recognizes the root cause of this cash flow problem, he still faces a tough time to change it. It takes a two-pronged approach.

First, the boss must realize the root cause is a personal habit that has affected his personal cash flow at home. Second, the boss must realize his bad personal habit has transferred to the company, causing poor cash management and cash flow issues. As the boss, we must be aware of our strengths and our risks, our good habits and our bad habits. I often say, "My wife is my best advisor!" I say that because she knows me better than I know myself. She sees and points out my good habits and bad habits, while I often only recognize my good habits and ignore the bad.

Having an honest advisor is a very valuable asset for the boss and the business. Bosses should surround themselves with people who know them well enough to offer honest and trusted critiques, at home as well as at work! For the boss to improve, he must first embrace his bad habits, own them, and strive to correct them.

Strive to make your habits good habits, for your sake, your family's sake, and for the sake of your business.

"WHEN YOU ASSUME NEGATIVE INTENT, YOU'RE ANGRY. IF YOU TAKE AWAY THAT ANGER AND ASSUME POSITIVE INTENT, YOU WILL BE AMAZED."

Indra Nooyi,
former CEO of PepsiCo

LESSON 23:
THE BOSS SHOULD STRIVE FOR POSITIVE OR NEUTRAL, NEVER NEGATIVE!

I RECEIVED A PHONE CALL FROM A BOSS WHO WAS struggling with a problem customer. I asked for more details and found out the rest of the story. This company provides its customers technical support and sells electronic equipment, which is often dependent on the internet.

The story went like this: their salesperson sold a big job with a lot of parts and man hours. The customer paid for half of the job in advance, which is standard for this industry. After a few trips to the customer's location, the job was not completed as the technicians discovered several problems; some were caused by the wrong parts being quoted for the job and some were because of the lack of internet connectivity.

The customer wanted the equipment pulled out and her down payment returned. The boss wanted to keep the down payment and was asking my opinion. I asked this question: "Was it possible to turn this negative into a neutral or positive experience for the customer?" I understood that a positive experience was a long shot, but a neutral experience could be achieved if the boss got involved.

My advice to the boss was for him to meet on-site with the customer and explain all that his company had done, which was a lot as they spent many man hours going back to the location to rectify the problem to no avail. The root cause of the problem was twofold: the company quoted the wrong equipment and poor internet. The boss needed to own these issues, at least regarding the wrong equipment, and own that they should have tested the internet connection prior to installing the equipment.

The boss going onto the customer's location was huge, as now you have two owners speaking together, both trying to solve a problem and make a profit. In these situations, I stress working to get to a neutral or positive position with the customer. The chances of a positive position where the customer writes a glowing testimonial was frankly not going to happen here; a neutral position, or the customer becoming content with the outcome, was the goal.

A customer who has a negative experience will talk about the negative over and over again. How do I know this? Because we do it in our daily lives. Think about a negative experience you may have had lately. What do you tell your family, friends, and frankly anyone else who will listen? We talk about the poor service or poor quality of the product we bought. We very seldom spend as much time talking about the great service or high-quality product we purchased lately. If we do this in our daily lives, we will do the same in our professional lives. We don't disconnect ourselves that way, we are who we are, always.

After a brief conversation, the boss concluded we could get to a neutral with this customer. The dollars invested to date in trying to rectify the situation were lost, so the dollars the boss was going to spend to get the customer to neutral were an investment—much like investing in advertising—trying to change a customer's perception from negative to neutral. At the end of the day the boss and the customer came to a neutral position and the negative in the market was silenced, at least in this case.

We are all in a competitive economy no matter what industry we operate in, every business must work hard to get and keep its customers. I stressed to the boss he needed to leave every conversation as either positive or neutral, never leave a conversation in a negative state. A negative can damage the company, as it will continue to resurface and may live a very long life. Positive or neutral is what we strive for, and the boss should not settle for anything less.

"WHEN MANAGEMENT AND LABOR (EMPLOYER AND EMPLOYEE) BOTH UNDERSTAND THEY ARE ALL ON THE SAME SIDE, THEN EACH WILL PROSPER MORE."

Zig Ziglar,
American Author and Motivational Speaker

LESSON 24:

THE BOSS IS NOT FAIR—FACT OR FICTION? YOU DECIDE...

WHEN I WORK IN AN ORGANIZATION, I GIVE my contact information to all employees who want it, and I encourage them to talk with me about anything in the organization they want. Also, when I visit the boss I ask for time to be set aside in case an employee wants a face-to-face with me.

During one visit, a department manager approached me and said, "Got a minute?" I said of course. We went into her office and closed the door. She told me the boss was unfair and did not treat everyone equally. I asked, "How so?" She began to explain that a peer of hers had just received a raise and she did not. I asked, "How do you know this?" She explained that everyone knew it, as if someone had broadcast it over the intercom!

I asked her if she was being paid what the boss promised her when she was hired. She answered that she was. I asked her if she was doing the best job possible as the manager of her department. She answered, "Yes, of course!" Then I said the agreement between her and the boss had not changed. You both are getting what was agreed upon when you were hired. She said she understood that, but why, then, did she not get a raise when the other person did? Again, I asked, "Are you absolutely sure this individual received a raise?" She answered she was pretty sure. I offered her a possible scenario to ponder.

Imagine the boss wanted to hire a person but wasn't sure he could do the job. The boss offered him a lower wage to start until the new employee was able to prove himself in the position. Once he proved himself, he would then receive the standard wage for the position—in essence a raise to the wage everyone else in his position was earning. She said that was possible, but she couldn't say for sure that it did happen. I added, "Or that it did not happen."

I suggested that she talk with the boss about her concerns, and then I offered her this advice. Imagine that when the boss interviews a new hire, he realizes what he is offering the potential employee the following: a living wage that will support a good lifestyle, a benefit package that will include health insurance and a retirement account, a good culture to grow in professionally, a safe environment to work in, and more. The boss is also thinking, "If I hire this person, how is he going to make me money? How is he going to improve my operation and increase the cash flow or profits of the business?" If the boss thought the new hire could not improve the operation, why would the boss hire him?

When you go to talk with the boss about a raise, ask yourself those questions. If you cannot answer them in a positive way, I suggest you wait on your request.

Think about the cash in the organization as a pie chart. If you cannot grow the chart by increasing the available cash, and the boss gives you a raise, that raise will shrink another slice of the pie, leaving less cash for others to work with. How could the boss grant your request under those circumstances?

I then offered one more tidbit. I told her that I tell all my young managers who have worked for me to always "trust but verify everything you hear, no matter who tells you!" In business, I have learned that often what is said is for the benefit of the person delivering the message…and they are looking out for themselves or others. This leaves you to look out for yourself!

Master Jedi Obi Wan Kenobi once said, "Everything is true—from a certain point of view." Trust what people say to you, but verify it before you believe it and act on it. This small piece of advice will serve you well throughout your career and in your life outside of work.

COMPANY CULTURE

"THE GREATEST LEADER IS NOT NECESSARILY THE ONE WHO DOES ALL THE GREAT THINGS. HE IS THE ONE THAT GETS THE PEOPLE TO DO THE GREAT THINGS."

Ronald Reagan,
40th President of the United States of America

LESSON 1:
ARE YOU LEADING YOUR ORGANIZATION TO ITS FULL POTENTIAL?

OFTEN I AM ASKED TO FACILITATE LEADERSHIP seminars for managers of organizations. One of the best books I have found for training managers in leadership is *The Leadership Secrets of Colin Powell* by Oren Harari. In this book, Colin Powell introduces the reader to his twelve leadership secrets. One of his leadership secrets is "being responsible sometimes means pissing people off."

In my career I have bought businesses, and in doing so, I have had to change cultures and assess the full potential of new employees who joined our team through acquisitions. One such employee was Mary (of course

Mary is not her real name). The company culture prior to the acquisition put a high value on the quantity of work an employee put out, not necessarily the quality of work. Mary had been with the previous owner for many years and was a valued employee because she did a lot of different tasks in the office. So many tasks that Mary was unable to do a majority of them accurately, but Mary's old boss rewarded her and other employees based on their volume of work.

The new culture I wanted to establish would value the quality of work an employee did along with a reasonable volume of work performed. I asked Mary to divide up some of her tasks among the other employees in the office and share her workload. Mary was trained over the years to be very controlling, and I recognized that if our new company was to reach its full potential, Mary would have to relinquish some of her duties, otherwise she would eventually become, if she was not already, our "glass ceiling", causing a bottleneck in our workflow.

Mary resisted my recommendations, and it caused stress in our organization. I came to realize I needed to take control and make a change. Mary was a very valuable employee as she knew almost every customer and a great deal about our processes. I knew I wanted to salvage her, and I also knew she was not happy working under these stressful conditions.

I took most of Mary's duties away from her, doing most of them myself as I knew it would be temporary until I could assess what her limits would be. She conformed but not without resenting my actions. In fact I would say she was royally pissed off at me. Once I established a baseline of tasks, I began to assign duties back to Mary one at a time, and I watched as she took on the tasks and performed them admirably until such time as she became overloaded again. I took back a few tasks until I was sure she could handle the workload at a high level of efficiency and accuracy. I would give her "positive strokes", as Kenneth Blanchard would say in his book *The One Minute Manager*, when I noticed she did a task correctly.

Before long, Mary was performing at a very high level, and I believe really enjoying her job. In the past Mary knew she was making more than the usual amount of mistakes, and I believe this caused her not to enjoy her job. I also knew that Mary was a diehard baseball fan and would listen to her favorite team's games on her break. I told Mary because she was doing such a good job that she could listen to the games at her desk during her work hours as long as it didn't affect her work. Mary was thrilled. Everyone else in the office was also thrilled because Mary had become a joy to work with.

As a leader of your organization sometimes you will be forced to piss people off. Remember to always preserve the employee's self-esteem and be kind. At the end of the day you must lead your organization and not let it run on autopilot if you want to reach your full potential. If you do it right, your employees will thank you for it.

Today I can honestly say that Mary and I are friends and we enjoy pleasant conversations when we run into each other in public.

"IF PEOPLE LIKE YOU,
THEY'LL LISTEN TO YOU, BUT
IF THEY TRUST YOU, THEY'LL
DO BUSINESS WITH YOU."

Zig Ziglar,
American Author and Motivational Speaker

LESSON 2:

HOW DO I BEGIN TO CHANGE FROM AN ENABLEMENT CULTURE TO AN ACCOUNTABILITY CULTURE?

IN THE PAST, I HAVE WRITTEN ABOUT THE CHALlenges facing business owners when they have an "enablement" culture verses an "accountability" culture. Recently I began working with a boss to change their company's enablement culture to an accountability culture.

I asked the six supervisors in this organization to list the eight most critical job duties of each of their direct reports. Then I asked the employees of these supervisors to list what they thought their eight most critical job duties were. In the next step we compared what the supervisors identified as critical and what their employees reported as their most critical.

In most cases the supervisors and direct reports were aligned on about five or six of the most critical job duties. This left us with an opportunity to improve efficiencies and workflow.

Efficiencies can be gained when employees understand what the boss sees as most critical to the company's success and, in turn, their own success. The other duties listed by employees, but not seen as most critical by the boss, were taking valuable time away from the truly critical duties necessary for the organization to reach its full potential. This does not mean the less critical duties are to be ignored—on the contrary they need to be done, but not at the expense of the critical job duties. Critical duties first, then other duties as time allows.

As we continued discussions with the supervisors and the employees we identified the inflows and outflows of the work process. One employee's outflows were another employee's inflows. A lack of outflows of critical duties from many employees upstream in the production process was causing a bottleneck in the production cycle downstream. The employees who were upstream did not understand what their teammates downstream needed and why.

We introduced the concept of internal customers and encouraged each employee to see the person next to them as an internal customer. This company had a great reputation for outstanding customer service and every employee knew the boss would accept nothing short of excellence when it came to customer service. Now we were taking customer service to the next level.

Once we got the eight critical duties in alignment within the production process, we began to list the tasks needed to complete each of the critical job duties. Each critical job duty included six to eight tasks needed to complete that duty efficiently. This process taught each employee what they needed to do to be successful in completing each critical job duty. It also communicated to each employee what the boss expected them to do on a daily, if not hourly, basis. Now the boss could hold the employees accountable to these tasks, which in turn made them accountable to each critical job duty.

These duties and tasks became part of the employees' job descriptions and were included in their performance evaluations conducted bi-annually by their supervisors. Performance-based raises were awarded depending on the quality of work as measured by these duties and tasks. The overall efficiencies of the organization improved, as employees now understood what was important and why their internal customer needed work to be done in a certain way. As you can imagine this process reduced costs.

The boss improved profitability of the organization without raising prices or chopping heads. *Good employees will do good work if they know what their job duties are and how to do the tasks associated with those duties.* Your employees are too valuable to your organization— it is your job to communicate to them what success looks like, then train, measure, and reward!

"INDIVIDUAL COMMITMENT
TO A GROUP EFFORT –
THAT IS WHAT MAKES A
TEAM WORK, A COMPANY
WORK, A SOCIETY WORK,
A CIVILIZATION WORK."

Vince Lombardi,
former American Football Coach

LESSON 3:
GIVE YOUR EMPLOYEES A FORUM TO IMPROVE COMMUNICATIONS

WHEN I ENTER AN ORGANIZATION, I AM CON-
sidered a "change agent," and the boss expects
things to be different after I have engaged with the
company. After a good bit of time observing the culture
and interviewing the employees, I set off to improve the
organization's profitability and ultimately the owner's
equity. I usually have a top five areas that I look at for
improvements. One of those areas is communications.

Recently I began working with an organization with
five department heads. I asked the boss how often they
meet as a group. He stated they did not and there was
no reason to as he had an open-door policy, and any

one of his people could come talk with him at any given time.

After more discussions I found the main reason was money. He ultimately said he calculated the hourly salary cost of each manager, and to have them all in one meeting at a time would be too expensive for the company as they were experiencing lean cash flow. I said I understand as I would do the same calculations in my companies, but I did not see the salaries as an expense but an investment.

After interviewing the department managers, I was told by more than one that, "No one really knows what I do here!" If that was true, how could this person really be appreciated for what he or she brought to the company? I recommended the boss have a monthly managers meeting with an agenda and a time limit to help control the investment that the boss would be making in his company.

The monthly meeting would be set up so each manager would have an opportunity to report on their departments as to what they did last month and what their plans were for the department this month. The managers would be doing most of the talking and, in a sense, reporting to the boss and the other managers their wins, losses, and challenges in their departments. This gave the managers a forum to communicate with each other that would spill over to their daily routines and begin to create enhanced teamwork and greater efficiencies between the managers in the organization.

I explained that this type of communication was different than what the boss offered in his open-door policy. The managers topics would be different between their peers than they were with the boss.

Now, this chapter speaks to the enhanced communications and teamwork that comes with this type of managers meeting, but it can also be tied to an improvement in accountability when it is accompanied by a balanced scorecard. By using a balanced scorecard, the managers would have metrics they would report on to the group. The boss could celebrate the wins and use the losses as a coaching moment for the entire group. The challenges, which would be highlighted on the balanced scorecard, would be a topic for all to contribute their ideas as they rally as a group to help each other develop solutions.

Communications beget teamwork, and teamwork begets improved efficiencies, which beget an improvement in owner's equity. Create a forum for your employees to talk to each other and improve your bottom line.

"GOOD BUSINESS LEADERS CREATE A VISION, ARTICULATE THE VISION, PASSIONATELY OWN THE VISION, AND RELENTLESSLY DRIVE IT TO COMPLETION."

Jack Welch,
former Chairman and CEO of General Electric

LESSON 4:
PERFECT CULTURE VERSES PERFECT JOB: CULTURE WINS EVERY TIME!

I HAVE HAD THE PRIVILEGE OF TEACHING MANY MBA students during my seventeen-year career as an adjunct faculty member. Often I am contacted by a past student as they search out career advice. One such request was from an MBA student who had gone on and earned her CPA credentials and was now looking to move on to other opportunities. That is what she initially told me, but after a few rotations of questions and answers I understood the underlying reason for her career move was deeper than she realized.

The root cause of her motivation to move on was due to the culture changing in her current organization. New management meant new rules and a new direction with a revised mission statement for the organization. These are all things you might expect with a change in leadership, but what I asked her to do was to line up the new mission statement with her own personal mission statement. Once she did that, it was obvious to both of us that her decision to look outside her organization for new opportunities was the right decision. She already had two opportunities at hand and wanted my advice as to the best fit for her.

She described the first company as a smaller family-owned business with approximately 100 employees and several business units which she would be responsible for developing the financials and managing the cash flow. Because it was a smaller company the annual salary was less than she was currently making. The second organization was a corporation that had over 300 employees and she would be the top finance person, be one of five people advising the CEO, and the annual salary was comparable to what she was earning today. We discussed the pros and cons of each position and at the end of our conversation I asked her to give me the good, the bad, and the ugly for each choice.

She said on paper the second company looked like the perfect job that would catapult her career and eventually satisfy her professional goals. I asked her to describe those job duties and she did in detail. I then asked her what was different between the responsibilities she had working for her current company and those she just described for the larger company choice. She just looked at me, smiled, and said, "Well nothing, I guess." I then asked, "So why are you thinking of leaving your perfect job?"

I explained to her that we are all smart people and most of us will leave our current job, not because we cannot perform the job duties but because we do not fit the culture. Whether we hired ourselves into a bad culture or that culture changed while we were employed with the company, we will leave because we no longer fit that culture.

I asked her which culture best fit her personal mission statement and told her to seriously consider that company and money should not be the deciding factor. I explained, "It wasn't the driving factor for why you are leaving your current company, and it should not be the driving factor of why you join another."

The boss creates a vision and develops the mission statement, then must drive that mission throughout the company. If the boss's new mission statement conflicts with your own personal mission statement, it is only a matter of time before you must leave! Embrace this as an opportunity and hire yourself into a culture that allows you to thrive, do good work, and most of all, to be happy.

"EVERYONE ON THE TEAM
PLAYS AN EQUAL ROLE.
MY ROLE IS TO CREATE
THE WAVE AND EVERYONE
ON THE TEAM KEEPS
THE WAVE GOING."

William Wang,
Founder and CEO of Vizio

LESSON 5:
BEGIN TO CHANGE THE CULTURE WITH WEEKLY MANAGERS MEETINGS.

A FTER A FEW MONTHS OF WORKING IN AN OR-
ganization and strategizing with the boss, I begin
to know the business in a more intimate manner. At
first, I want to understand the operations of the business to determine if the organization has a sustainable
business model to build upon. I also begin to have
extended conversations with the employees, beginning
with the department heads and then the rank-and-file
employees. By doing so I begin to understand the company culture.

I determine if the culture is a healthy culture or if the
culture is hindering the business in any way. I often find

company cultures to be either one of accountability or one of enablement. If the culture is one of accountability, it is much easier to accomplish the boss's goals for the business. If the culture is one of enablement, I often find an atmosphere of blame and mistrust between the boss, management, and the employees.

If a culture of enablement exists, change is necessary. Change of responsibilities and often change of staff. Everyone is encouraged to accept the changes the boss and I implement as we move toward a culture of accountability. This change can result in some employees selecting to leave the organization, mostly because they are the ones who are enabled and often are protective of their entitled status. The boss must support the change, or the change will not be successful. If the boss is hesitant to accept and adapt to the change, I often negotiate a time limit for the change to show results and ask the boss to use newly established data and metrics when determining if the process is working.

As the culture begins to change (and it will) the department managers start to see their efforts pay off and their employees thrive in the new culture, resulting in more positive attitudes among employees. This is not a quick fix and can take some time—the boss must understand this. I explain this process to the boss by using the following example.

Changing a culture from one of blame and mistrust to one of encouragement and teamwork is slow going. It is like turning an ocean liner. It is slow going until the vessel is pointed in the new direction, and then it can pick up speed and gain momentum with little effort. The boss is often used to making quick decisions and expecting fast results. This is akin to the boss riding a jet ski and doing circles around our ocean liner. Having the patience to realize the benefits of the team's efforts is the most challenging for the boss. I can assure the boss that patience will pay off in increased profits, resulting in increased owner's equity.

In order to reinforce the changes, weekly managers meetings are established, and in these meeting the boss has ten minutes to give an overview of the company. This stops the boss from dominating the conversations. This meeting is not for the boss but for improved communications and team building between department managers.

Next, each department manager has ten minutes to give an overview of their department. They will be expected to report on what's coming for the week, what's working well, and what's frustrating them. The boss encourages the team to suggest solutions to the various problems, always stating that the department manager must make the final decision, as he or she will be responsible for the results. This will increase communications and begin to get the team working together.

Celebrating small wins is made easy in this type of environment. Problems are shared and solutions are discussed among the managers. The individual managers begin to use the management team as their advisory team, helping each other develop solutions to their problems or challenges. I have seen this happen, and when it works it can drive profits at an exponential rate.

"EVERYONE TALKS ABOUT BUILDING A RELATIONSHIP WITH YOUR CUSTOMERS. I THINK YOU SHOULD BUILD ONE WITH YOUR EMPLOYEES FIRST."

Angela Ahrendts,
Vice President of Apple

LESSON 6:
CONTROL WHAT YOU CAN CONTROL, INFLUENCE WHAT YOU CAN INFLUENCE.

I WAS ASKED BY THE BOSS OF A FAMILY-OWNED business to help him control his employee turnover. I reviewed his financials and found a mediocre profit, but everything looked to be in order. The next step was to look inside his organization.

I spent time with his department heads, and after some time I began to understand the root cause of the problem. It often takes a little time for me to get the real stories from the employees because at first they see me as an extension of the boss. I have even been told that I am "in the boss's back pocket." After a few conversations, this myth is dispelled as I tell all my clients from the boss down that I do not work for the boss, I work for the company. If I must tell the boss he or she is wrong, so be it. This encourages more candid and honest conversations with the employees, who, by the way, usually know the problem and have a good idea what a solution should be.

In this organization the boss had family members working in the business. In the eyes of the employees they had special privileges and could do no wrong. I asked the employees if the family members were good at their jobs, and in most cases their job performance was not an issue; their entitled attitudes were the problem and the reason most past employees left the company. According to the current employees the boss was unfair and favored his family over his employees. When I discussed this with the boss, he agreed that this was the case.

The boss was a second-generation owner who became the boss of the company when his father passed. He felt he had a huge responsibility to keep the company going, to support the family members working at the company, and to support his mother, who was still receiving a salary from the company, although she had not worked there for years.

I explained my view of his turnover problem and the lack of profitability it caused. The problem was one of inequity and a lack of respect for the boss's management style. The solution was for the boss to understand that the foundation of his business was his employees.

I asked the boss if he could talk to every customer every day. Of course, he said he could not, which meant the boss had less influence over his customers than he did over his employees. I explained he could talk with every employee every day to encourage them, motivate them, and show them they are valued! By talking with each employee daily he would create a stronger relationship with them, and they would feel more loyalty to him and the company. In essence, "The employees would do what the boss needed them to do and like it!" The boss needed to see his employees as the future of his business and focus on them, not family security—that security would come as a result of a greater employee focus.

I believe the boss was granting privileges to his family members as a substitute for the financial security he felt he was not providing them. This was damaging to the business's culture and the main cause of his employee turnover problem, which in turn was eating away at his profits. The boss needed to invest more of his time in the foundation of his company, his employees, in turn the employees would offer an awesome buying experience to his customers, who in turn would provide the financial security for his family.

Bottom line, the boss understood holding himself accountable would be a first step to lowering the employee turnover, improving profitability, and establishing security for his family.

"ACCOUNTABILITY:
THE GLUE THAT TIES
COMMITMENT TO RESULTS."

Bob Proctor,
Canadian self-help author and lecturer

LESSON 7:
CULTURE: ENABLEMENT OR ACCOUNTABILITY?

THE BUSINESS OWNER, THE BOSS, ESTABLISHES the culture in an organization. It can be a culture of enablement or a culture of accountability. Often when I am asked to help with a company, I discover the culture is one of enablement. Even worse, the boss is the worst enabler of them all. Enablement hurts productivity, causes safety issues, and undermines company morale. Here is an example that drives the lesson home.

I was working in my office one day and I got a call from Dave, who was our area OSHA representative I knew well. It is important to get to know these people before they show up at your door for an official visit. I knew Dave from some volunteer work we did together for the area YMCA. He was a good guy and we were on a first-name basis.

Well, he called me to tell me he was sitting in his office looking out the window and saw one of my service technicians working in the bucket truck, fixing a lighting fixture. He said the technician had his lanyard hooked to his belt, not the bucket. Of course this was an OSHA violation and that was why Dave was calling. I said I wanted to meet him on-site, and so we did. Come to find out the technician was Jim, a twelve-year veteran and the head of my installation and service crews.

Fast-forward, I laid off Jim for five days without pay, according to our employee handbook rules, and worked with Dave to lower my OSHA fine to $5,000. I could have left Jim off the hook with a warning, but what message would I have sent to the other crew members and every other employee in the company? The message they got was, "If the boss laid off Jim, he would have no problem laying me off, so I had better stay clean and mind the rules." Did it cost me more than the $5,000 fine? Sure it did, as I lost one of my top guys for five days. But in the long run I felt I saved future dollars, and more important, I might have prevented one of my employees from being injured or worse.

If I had let Jim off with a slap on the wrist, I would have been enabling all other employees to bend the rules and potentially cause the company a larger exposure in the future. I would have been undermining my efforts to create a culture of accountability and avoid a culture of enablement.

It is important that you enforce the rules equally across the board—what is good for one is good for all. As the boss you set the culture, so what is your call? Enablement or accountability, it's your choice.

`"THE LEADER IS ONE WHO
KNOWS THE WAY, GOES THE
WAY, AND SHOWS THE WAY."

John C. Maxwell,
American Author, and Speaker

LESSON 8:
THE BOSS NEEDS TO LEAD FROM THE FRONT OF THE HERD.

I MEET A LOT OF BUSINESS OWNERS WITH VARY-ing leadership styles. According to the employees I interview, one of the most frustrating styles is the boss who leads from the center of the herd. What do I mean by this? Most bosses would like to have a team of thoroughbreds. These are the people who are the best at what they do. They are confident, innovative, and at the ready to do their jobs. If the boss wants to keep these individuals motivated and engaged, they need to lead from the front of the herd.

Imagine a herd of stallions running in the wild. The lead stallion is running in the center of the herd, and the herd is running full stride toward a cliff. By the time the lead stallion identifies the danger, the front half of the herd has already fallen to their doom. If the lead stallion had been leading from the front of the herd, this most likely would not have happened. That lead stallion needs to be the boss.

The boss is the person who sets the vision for the company as it moves into the future. If the boss does not do this, or worse yet sets the vision and then changes it day by day depending on what has happened in the past twenty-four hours, the thoroughbreds will leave the herd. They leave because they can! Others of lessor abilities do not leave as readily because they may feel they could not make it in another organization or they are just too comfortable to make the change, but those thoroughbreds do not feel this way. They are confident and know the value of their abilities. Therefore they need a strong leader who leads from the front of the herd.

The boss may be frustrated with the performance of the company, in the financial performance or in the lack of efficiencies. The boss often cannot figure out why the thoroughbreds are not performing to the best of their abilities. In these cases, I often find that the boss is not leading the organization. The boss may be an absentee owner—this is the worst scenario. In most cases, an absentee owner is a recipe for failure. Even if the boss is around half of the time, without the full picture this often causes more problems than any benefits the boss may bring when engaged.

Some of the best bosses solicit the opinions from their thoroughbreds and establish ownership in team decisions. The boss may only have 25% of the information at the time but moves forward in a direction identified by the team. Under the leadership of the boss the team understands they may have to pivot when more information is available. When 50% and 75% of the information becomes available, the boss along with the team may see the need to pivot and change direction again. Eventually, 100% of the information becomes available, and by this time the competition is ready to move forward. By leading from the front, the boss has the team ahead of the competition, and the thoroughbreds are running full stride into the future.

Lead from the front of the herd by being the leader your thoroughbreds are looking for, and then let them loose to benefit your company.

FINANCIAL LITERACY

"BUSINESS MUST BE RUN AT A PROFIT; ELSE IT WILL DIE. BUT WHEN ANYONE TRIES TO RUN BUSINESS SOLELY FOR PROFIT, THEN ALSO THE BUSINESS MUST DIE, FOR IT NO LONGER HAS A REASON FOR EXISTENCE."

Henry Ford,
Founder of the Ford Motor Company

LESSON 1:
PROFITABLE BUSINESS MODEL FIRST, MARKETING SECOND

A FRIEND OF MINE WHO OWNED A RESTAURANT on the north side of town called me and asked if I would stop by because he had a few questions. I agreed, and when my schedule allowed I planned to stop in to his restaurant (close to lunchtime because he had great food).

I met with him and his wife, who both worked in the business at the time. He said his sales were down and he wanted to ask me questions about how he could increase his sales. I asked, as I usually do, if I could see a financial statement. He showed me his year-to-date profit and loss statement. I did a few calculations and said it looked like he was working very hard generating little profit. He said things were going okay and all he needed was more sales. At that time his wife, who I sensed was getting frustrated with her husband, began to tell me how they were working too hard, not making any money, and it was making life difficult at home also. Eventually my friend agreed that they were struggling.

I did some more calculations and suggested to my friend that he should raise his main entrees at least by a one dollar each if he wanted to make any money at all. He said he couldn't do that because it would cost him too many customers. We agreed to disagree and I left without committing to anything. I did get a really nice lunch though.

A few months later I received another call from my friend asking if I would stop in when I had a few minutes. I stopped in to the restaurant a few days later and he showed me a menu with most of his entrees priced a one dollar higher than before. I asked him how that was working for him and he stated his sales dropped off by 15% but he was making more money than he had ever made before. I suggested that the customers who stayed were staying because he has great food and the customer who left were only there because the prices were too cheap. He asked, "Now what do we do to make even more profits?" We began to set a strategy to drive more customers into the restaurant because now he had a profitable business model to work with.

Driving sales is not always the first step to increasing profitability. A business owner must have a profitable business model first, otherwise you are going to end up working harder only to lose even more money than you did before. Honestly we probably would not have gotten to this point if his wife had not gotten frustrated with our conversation and told me what was really happening.

As businesses owners we have to understand that admitting that something is broken is the first step in developing a fix to the problem.

"YOU CANNOT CHANGE YOUR DESTINATION OVERNIGHT, BUT YOU CAN CHANGE YOUR DIRECTION OVERNIGHT."

Jim Rohn,
former Entrepreneur, Author, and Speaker

LESSON 2:
DOES YOUR COMPANY HAVE A GPS, AND IF SO, DO YOU USE IT?

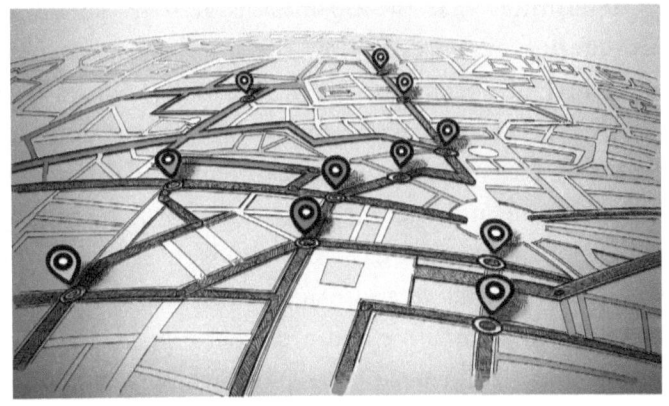

A FEW YEARS AGO I BOUGHT A GPS FOR MY CAR and I liked it so much I bought one for my wife's car also. Eventually we got GPS service on our smart phones and we tend to us that GPS more often. I recently bought a car that has a GPS as a standard option and I like it even more. It works best when there is a detour or when I am going to a new client's office and I don't want to waste time guessing what route to take.

In Q4 or early in Q1 I work with my clients to create an annual operating budget. We look at past performance, we look at all costs (valid numbers will work the best, but don't let iffy numbers stop you), we look at revenues because most business owners will track revenue fairly accurately but may fall short on tracking operating costs. We identify profit centers for the business and determine the gross profit per profit center the best we can with the data we have. The more valid the past data the more accurate the pro forma annual budget can be.

We determine what the business is actually spending on operating expenses "below the line." *Below the line* is a term I use often and it includes all expenses that are not captured in cost of goods sold. This is done on a monthly basis to determine seasonality of the operation's revenue, net income, and cash flow. Eventually we develop an annual cash flow budget, allowing the owner to be proactive and react to any cash flow situations as soon as possible and often before they happen. This is great information to have when strategizing with your banker.

One of the biggest benefits to having this operating budget is planning where you want to take your business in the next twelve months, much like using a GPS to plan your next trip. The annual budget helps the business owner react when there is a detour in the master plan. Seeing how a changing market affects your financial performance and having the information to pivot early can prove very valuable.

The first iteration of your operating budget may not be the most accurate, but the business owner will find that the current actual data collected to compare to the annual budget is going to be more accurate because the business owner is paying more attention to the numbers on a monthly schedule.

Not having an annual operating budget is like driving without a GPS. Worse yet, having an annual budget and not using it, after a few weeks or a few months, because the business owner perceives that "other things are more important" is like having a GPS, putting in the route, and not using the GPS as you drive. Most people wouldn't take a trip without a GPS once they have used one.

Do you have a GPS for your business, and if so, do you use it? Your GPS is your annual operating budget. Are you actually executing your plan on a daily basis? The most profitable businesses I know have an annual operating budget and annual cash flow budget and understand how the daily decisions on the shop floor or in the office will affect the financials compared to that budget. Every decision is a financial decision when it comes to establishing accountability to the actual verses budget report.

It is never too late to start developing your annual operating budget and your annual cash flow budget.

"ANY GOOD BUSINESS PERSON APPLIES FINANCIAL DISCIPLINE TO EVERYTHING THEY DO."

Paula Wagner,
Film Producer & Executive

LESSON 3:

UNDERSTANDING FINANCIALS: AS EASY AS RIDING A BICYCLE?

I MAGINE BEING INTRODUCED TO A BICYCLE FOR the first time as an adult. You are told all you have to do is hop on and start pedaling, it's easy! You think about it and you have your doubts. After all, you have had classes on Newton's Law of Gravity and you understand that the force that caused the apple's acceleration (gravity) must be dependent upon the mass of the apple. Common sense tells you that with your mass, you will hit the ground hard when you tip either to the left or the right. Yet you see small children enjoying riding their bicycles without falling. How does this work? The rider should tip and fall. This riding a bicycle thing just doesn't make sense.

It won't make sense until you are taught how to ride the bicycle and, more importantly, until you believe you can balance on the bicycle and not fall to either side.

I am suggesting you think of financials like riding a bicycle—they will not make sense until you are taught how they work and, more importantly, until you believe you can understand them. I have worked with several artists who own their own businesses. They often tell me they will never understand financials and they explain to me that "it's a left brain, right brain thing." I say nonsense, and once they are taught how the financials work, they get excited and very interested in their company's financials because they now understand the numbers and what the financials are telling them about the performance of their businesses.

If you do not fully understand the financials of your organization, you are putting your business at risk. It is your responsibility to educate yourself on the three main financial statements: the profit and loss statement, the balance sheet, and the cash flow statement. Most owners I work with who are very technical look at the profit and loss as the holy grail of the financials when in reality it is number three on the list. Don't get me wrong, the profit and loss will tell you how your monthly operations are doing, but as the business owner, you are responsible for the financial health of the company, and that information is found on the balance sheet and cash flow statement.

Every once in a while I meet with someone who is thinking about starting a business of their own. I ask them, "Have you ever been responsible for the financials of an organization?" They often answer, "Yes." I then ask, "Did you write out the checks and manage the cash flow?" They often answer, "No, the owner did that stuff, but I ran the business and always had a good profit and loss statement." It is at this time I must explain to the person that unless they have managed the cash flow of an organization and understand the balance sheet, they really haven't had the experience I feel they need before they invest their hard-earned dollars into starting or buying a business.

As business owners we know you don't invest more money into a business than you are willing to lose or can afford to lose if the organization goes south. This is just reality. One way to protect your owner's equity is to fully understand your financials. If you can't ride that financial bicycle today, you need to hop on and get educated. Don't let excuses such as "it's a left brain, right brain thing" or "a fear of falling off" stop you! You will enjoy your business a lot more once you fully understand what the financials are telling you.

"A BUDGET IS TELLING
YOUR MONEY WHERE TO GO
INSTEAD OF WONDERING
WHERE IT WENT."

Dave Ramsey,
American Radio Show Host, Author, and Businessman

LESSON 4:
AN ESSENTIAL TOOL FOR BUSINESS DURING GOOD TIMES AND BAD!

B ACK IN THE DAY, AS I AM TOLD I SAY WAY TOO often, a full-blown business plan would be necessary to get funding and, some may say, to have a successful business. Today times have changed, and that twenty-plus page business plan has become somewhat obsolete. What has replaced it? A three-year financial projection with eight to ten pages describing how the boss is going to execute to achieve the pro forma numbers.

In one of my past careers, I worked in an entrepreneurship center where we helped entrepreneurs launch approximately 170 new businesses over four years. What I saw were many of these new businesses going out of business in about eighteen to twenty-four months after launching. After closer investigation we noted that the new business could not create cash flow after the start-up funding was used up, causing the businesses to fail. That old adage is true: you can have profits without cash flow and go out of business, you can have cash flow without profits and fight another day!

If you want to know your business intimately, create a three-year operating budget with a very detailed first year and two following years of projections. At the end of the first year of operations, the old second year budget is reviewed and changes are made to any profit centers that need to be adjusted. The revised second year is promoted to the current year as the new operations budget, the old third year is promoted to the new second year and a new third year is created. With this method, the boss is always thinking three years out and has a detailed plan that can be used as a benchmark for operations as more information is collected throughout the year.

This type of budgeting becomes even more important when the economy weakens or a recession is looming beyond the horizon. Back in 2008 if the boss had this type of budgeting in place, he would adjust the pro forma and pivot for the business to survive. I do not recommend changing a budget after it has been accepted and distributed to funding sources, but when extenuating circumstances arise, the boss must react.

Using financial software, I encourage the boss to look at the actual verses budget mid-month to estimate what the final revenues and net income will be for the month. This proactive approach allows the boss to adjust the operations to embrace stronger sales trends or to adjust costs when revenues are not going to track as expected.

Don't be the boss who is looking at their revenues and profits from last month on the fifteenth of this month, which puts you in a total reactive mode. By reviewing the actual against the budget numbers mid-month, the boss becomes proactive and can do something to affect the outcome.

The boss is a risk taker by nature, always looking for new opportunities and the next big thing. As a risk taker, the boss needs to be proactive and secure the core business model against competition and a global economy. Protecting the core business allows the boss the freedom to take risks. No one has a crystal ball, but a good three-year pro forma budget will substitute nicely.

"DO NOT FOCUS ON MONEY, INSTEAD FOCUS ON A PROBLEM THAT NEEDS TO BE SOLVED FOR THE WORLD."

Manoj Arora,
IT Executive and Author

LESSON 5:
ARTISTS, MUSICIANS, AND FINANCIALS, OH MY! DOESN'T HAVE TO BE SCARY.

I WAS INVITED TO PRESENT AT A SELF-EMPLOY-ment in the arts conference where my audience was artists, musicians, and other self-employed artist types in a variety of fields. My topic was "Financials and the Arts". I have experience presenting on financial literacy to executive directors of nonprofits, so I had a sense of the relationship between understanding the mission of an organization and understanding the financials of an organization. These artists had a very strong sense of mission, not much of finance.

I began by explaining the three financial statements. The profit and loss statement is like your paycheck. If you worked forty hours a week at $10 an hour, your take home pay was not $400, it was less taxes, insurances, and other deductions. This is how the profit and loss statement works. Your revenue minus your expenses, and then you get to take home the difference in the form of profits.

Your cash flow statement works like your personal debit card. If you have money in your account, you can draw funds from your debit card or pay bills with it. You don't have to put money into your debit card account every day in order to use it every day. When you run out of money, the balance is zero, and your debit card will not work. Cash flow in your business works the same way. If your company has a positive cash balance in the bank you can write checks or use your company's debit card, if your balance is zero, you will not be able to use the company debit card until you deposit more funds into the company bank account. "Cash is king" is a phrase all business owners will learn to appreciate.

Your company balance sheet is like your mortgage on your home. You may have a home worth $150,000. You will invite a friend over and say, "Come on over to my house and we can paint together." If you have a mortgage, you do not own the entire house. For example, you owe $100,000 on your mortgage, which means your equity is $50,000; in other words, you own one-third of your home and the bank that holds the mortgage owns two-thirds of your home. The company balance sheet works the same way. It tells what percentage of the company the business owner owns and what percentage of the company the bank owns.

One last concept I try to drive home is that financials are only a reflection of the business. If you want to improve the financials you have to adjust the business operations to effect the change. An example I use is "The Bean" in Chicago. If you Google The Bean you will see a silver bean with reflections of the Chicago skyline on it. If you wanted to change the images on The Bean you cannot wipe them off with a rag, you will have to change the Chicago skyline to change the reflections on The Bean. Financials work the same way—you cannot just change the numbers on your financials to show a profit, you will have to improve the operations to show a profit. Financials are a reflection of reality and cannot be changed unless you change the reality.

You do not need to be an accountant to own a business. I appreciate fine art, but you wouldn't want to commission a painting from me, I have zero artistic talent! Likewise, I may not want you doing the financials for my business. As a business owner you need to know enough to know when something is wrong. Then you can seek out a financial professional to help correct the issues. You are a subject matter expert in your field, learn to seek out other subject matter experts to benefit your business.

"IF YOU DON'T UNDERSTAND FINANCIAL STATEMENTS, PEOPLE WILL DUMB DOWN THE CONVERSATION OR EXCLUDE YOU ALTOGETHER."

Gary Vaughan, Educator,
Author, Speaker, and Entrepreneur

LESSON 6:
FINANCIAL LITERACY IS A MUST!

OVER THE YEARS I HAVE WORKED WITH A LOT of various business owners of for-profit organizations and executive directors of nonprofit organizations. One common struggle I see in most organizations is a lack of financial intelligence caused by the lack of financial literacy.

Imagine if you were in a conversation and everyone around you spoke a language you did not understand. It would be impossible for you to fully participate in any conversation. Now imagine if you knew only a few words of that language. If others in the conversation understood your lack of vocabulary they would naturally limit the conversation to elementary words and phrases.

This is exactly what happens when business owners and executive directors don't understand the language of finance. Honestly, how can anyone expect you to understand a language that you have not been taught? It's up to you to educate yourself and your organization in the language of finance. A great book that you can share with your key decision-makers in your organization is *Financial Intelligence for Entrepreneurs* by Karen Berman and Joe Knight.

I often hear, "That damn banker didn't give me the loan again!" I usually ask the business owner if they thanked their banker for not doing so. They look at me as if I'm offering them a wise-ass comment. I then talk about the fourteen financial ratios I use to evaluate the health of a business. After we calculate these ratios for their business and I explain what they mean, the business owner has a better understanding as to why the banker did not offer the loan and oftentimes can better appreciate the banker's perspective.

If business owners understand what ratios the bankers and investors use to evaluate the health of a business, the better negotiating position the business owner has when they go to secure outside funding. If the banker does not offer a loan, ask them why. What ratios would they like to see improved? How can they help you achieve those goals? Learn to use your banking relationship as an asset for your business. The more engaged your banker is as you develop a plan to secure the funding you need, the better chance you have to achieve that funding. If your banker is not willing to engage, then find a better banker. Your banker, like your CPA and your lawyer, should be advisors to you and your business.

Financial literacy doesn't only pertain to the profit and loss statement, balance sheet, and cash flow statement, it also relates to the financial ratios and other measurements used by the finance industry. No matter what industry, no matter if you run a for-profit or nonprofit business, no matter if you have one employee or dozens, financial intelligence is a must and not just for business owners. Your key employees need to understand how their day-to-day decisions affect the monthly financials. It is our responsibility as business owners to help develop the financial intelligence of our organizations, and that starts with financial literacy.

HUMAN RESOURCES

"SOME PEOPLE WANT IT TO HAPPEN. SOME WISH IT TO HAPPEN. OTHERS MAKE IT HAPPEN."

Michal Jordan,
American Businessman, and former Professional Basketball Player

LESSON 1:
MEET YOUR EMPLOYEES WHERE THEY ARE FOR BETTER RESULTS.

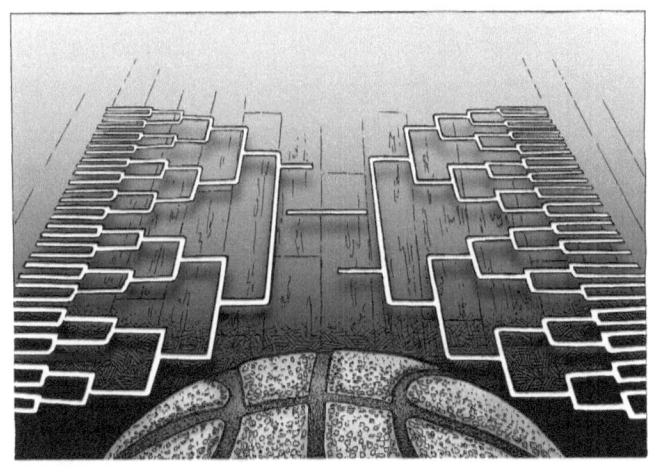

I RECENTLY HAD A CONVERSATION WITH THE BOSS regarding one of his younger employees who was an underachiever. I asked if I could talk with the lad and see if I could help to motivate the young man to improve his work ethics. The boss agreed and the conversation went something like this.

We were in the middle of March Madness and I asked if the young employee had ever played any sports. He said he was on the basketball team in high school. I asked what position he played, and he said he was the starting guard on the team. I then asked how his bracket was going. It was early in the tournament, and he said his bracket was blown up by Kentucky losing to St. Peter's. I said mine too!

I told him I was also a Badger fan, and they didn't help my bracket by exiting as early as they did. We chatted sports for a while and eventually got down to the topics that needed to be addressed. I must say that I am partial to hiring athletes and folks who have been raised on a farm. Farmers understand responsibility and hard work from young on. They also understand what it is to run a family business and the hardships that can go along with that lifestyle. I like hiring athletes because they know how to win and know how to get up and come back from adversity after a loss. They understand the value to teamwork and can take direction better than most.

During our conversation the young man took responsibility for not putting out the amount of effort the boss expected. He knew the boss was not happy with him and he did try to give a few flimsy reasons for not working up to what we both knew was his full potential.

Toward the end of the conversation I said, "I want you to think back to when you were on the basketball team. If you put C-level work into practice, you were folding towels. If you put B work into practice, you were sitting on the bench watching the other guys play. If you put A work in, you were the starting guard on the team."

I explained that his job was like being on the basketball team, except that B and C effort would get him off the team and looking for another job. A-level effort would get him the respect of the boss, and who knows what opportunities that would bring. I then challenged him to put as much effort into his job as he did to get that starting position on the basketball team. He looked at me with a weak smile and said he totally understood.

We ended the conversation by giving each other our picks for the final four and away he went back to work. I explained our conversation to the boss and asked him to watch the employee to see if there was any change in his effort. Days later when I spoke with the boss again, he said he was more than pleasantly surprised that the young man was really trying and doing much better. The boss and I had a conversation regarding gaining a rapport with his employees and meeting the younger generation where they are in life and with examples they can relate to.

The boss should always be looking for that win-win opportunity with the latest generation of workers. In today's competitive work environment, we must try to retain our employees and coach them to the level we need them to be. The cost of attracting and retaining employees is high, especially when the supply is low and demand is high.

If the boss can meet his employees where they are and coach them to the level needed, the company has a better chance to improve efficiencies, lower direct labor costs, and ultimately achieve a high owner's equity. Meeting your employees where they are and coaching them to their full potential is just good business.

"NOTHING WILL KILL A GREAT EMPLOYEE FASTER THAN WATCHING YOU TOLERATE A BAD ONE."

Perry Belcher,
Co-Founder Digitalmarketer.com

LESSON 2:
"WE GOT TO GET SHIT DONE AND WE CAN'T AFFORD TO LOSE ANYONE!"

I RECENTLY BEGAN TO WORK WITH A COMPANY that had a problem with employees not showing up for shifts and/or often leaving shifts early. We called a meeting of the management team and began to discuss the problem and how to correct this type of damaging behavior. I asked the boss if the company had a disciplinary policy and the proper forms for the managers to use to correct these types of activities. The boss said no, the company never had anything like that. The boss said in the old days he would just threaten to fire any employee the next time "stuff like this" happened, and that would be enough to correct the problem. As of the date when I wrote this, with the unemployment rate so low, the boss said he was afraid to discipline anybody because of the worker shortage, and as the boss said, "We got to get shit done and we can't afford to lose anyone!"

As we continued our discussion, the boss was not comfortable saying anything to the employee because he was afraid to lose another worker. I stressed the fact that at least disciplining the employee or even letting the employee go would be the best action the boss could take. He argued the fact that the company had a backlog of work and he didn't have people breaking down his door to work at his company. I continued to talk about efficiencies and the "good" employees having to work harder to make up for the "bad" employees he kept at the company.

As we continued the dialog his department managers joined in, and to the boss's surprise they were in favor of "firing" the employee and were also in favor of initiating a disciplinary policy they could use to manage their people.

I recommended templates I use, including disciplinary action forms, performance evaluation forms, and job descriptions. I coached the department managers as to how best to administer these new management tools. Eventually we created an employee manual that became part of their culture. As you can imagine the "good" employees really appreciated the structure and accountability, and the so called "bad" employees self-selected out of the company. The boss was also amazed that the efficiencies in the company increased and the morale of his employees improved.

Setting rules in place and administrating the rules fairly can make a huge difference in the culture of any company. The boss's greatest fear of *losing all his employees* was not realized but greater productivity was. Offering your managers the proper tools and coaching them how to use the tools makes good business sense and can increase profits without increasing prices.

"LEADERS DON'T CREATE
MORE FOLLOWERS. LEADERS
CREATE MORE LEADERS."

Tom Peters,
American Author

LESSON 3:
PEOPLE AND ALUMINUM ARE DIFFERENT, GO FIGURE!

A FEW YEARS AGO I WAS COACHING AN OWNER of a fabrication business. He is one of the smartest people I know and a very talented fabricator of aluminum products. I watched as he created precision bends and welds on the materials he used in his trade. He had a very good business, but he did have a challenge with keeping good people. I was hired to help him understand why he had such high turnover rates, which as you know costs the organization time and money.

One day I witnessed him speaking harshly to an employee. After the fact we talked about what spurred his emotions with that individual. In fact, I was told by other employees that this type of behavior from the boss was commonplace and was one of the main reasons people left the company. The owner explained how frustrated he was that he had to tell his people again and again before they understood what he wanted on the fabrication floor.

I asked him to bring me a piece of scrap aluminum, which he did. It was approximately a foot by a foot square. I asked him to bend the aluminum to a 90° angle, so he did. I then placed it next to his computer and said we would talk about why later.

The next day we went into his office and looked at the piece of aluminum. We talked about how the piece was still bent at that 90° angle and hadn't changed. I explained that his people aren't like this piece of aluminum, a material that he'd worked with most of his career. The aluminum doesn't go flat overnight, doesn't misunderstand that it should stay bent. People often times need to be told and/or shown a new task over and over again until they experience that ah-ha moment and finally get it! His employee turnover problem was a symptom of a greater challenge: unclear and/or poor communications.

I asked the owner to remember this piece of aluminum and think twice before getting frustrated with his people. When on the shop floor I could just say,

"He isn't a piece of aluminum," and the owner would immediately adjust his tone and explain again what he was looking for and why.

A few years after we stopped working together I visited him in his shop and he took me into his office to show me he still had that piece of aluminum on his desk. It was his "trophy" as he bragged to me that he had very little turnover in staff and was doing very well. I congratulated him and he let me buy him lunch!

"A BOSS HAS A TITLE. A LEADER HAS THE PEOPLE."

Simon Sinek,
American Author, and Motivational Speaker

LESSON 4:
WHO ARE YOUR "LEADERS WITHOUT STRIPES"?

Wh:N I AM ASKED by business owners to assist with changing the culture within their organization, I often ask, "Do you know who your 'leaders without stripes' are?" Business owners are some of the most prolific idea people within the  organization. They are constantly coming up with innovative ways to improve their businesses. While working with one business owner to change the culture in his organization I observed the following exchange.

The business owner delivered a speech to the organization describing a new policy to improve their culture. A young apprentice was walking back to his department after this meeting and asked his foreman, "What do you think? I think the boss has a great idea there." The foreman had been with the company for a long time and had seen a lot of "stuff" come and go within the organization. His response to the young apprentice was, "Listen, you work for me! This is another one of the boss's ideas that will fizzle out in a week or two. You do what I tell you or you'll answer to me!" The young apprentice agreed and stepped in line with his foreman.

The question becomes, "Who is really leading the company?" There is little chance the culture will change in this scenario. How would you use this experienced foreman, your "leader without stripes", to be an advocate for the change? Let's look…

Take two:

The boss asks for a meeting with the foreman prior to his announcement. He asks the old sage for his advice on how to initiate a new idea regarding the culture of the company. The business owner offers two scenarios and asks the experienced foreman which one he thinks would work best. (It is important that both scenarios are acceptable to the business owner at this point. The business owner should not offer a scenario that he does not agree with or want.) The foreman recommends the one he is most comfortable with.

Let's relook at the exchange between the young apprentice and his foreman.

After the boss's speech the young apprentice was walking back to his department with his foreman and asked, "What do you think? I think the boss has a great idea there." The foreman's new response goes something like this. "Listen, where do you think the boss got that great idea? He got it from ME and if you don't fall in and get behind MY new policy you'll deal with me!" The young apprentice smiles at the old foreman—the young guy knows the foreman likes to sound tough but is really a softy at heart and will vigorously defend his guys. Because of this relationship the apprentice is loyal to his foreman, loyal to a point where he would walk through fire for the old guy. This is why in most cases the apprentice will take his marching orders from his foreman, who will trump the boss every time.

If you want to change a culture or initiate a major new policy within your organization you must understand who the "leaders without stripes" are and get them on board with your plans before you announce them, otherwise you have the potential to waste time and money.

"YOUR MISSION STATEMENT BECOMES YOUR CONSTITUTION, THE SOLID EXPRESSION OF YOUR VISION AND VALUES."

Steven Covey,
former Educator, Author, Businessman, and Speaker

LESSON 5:
MISSION STATEMENT

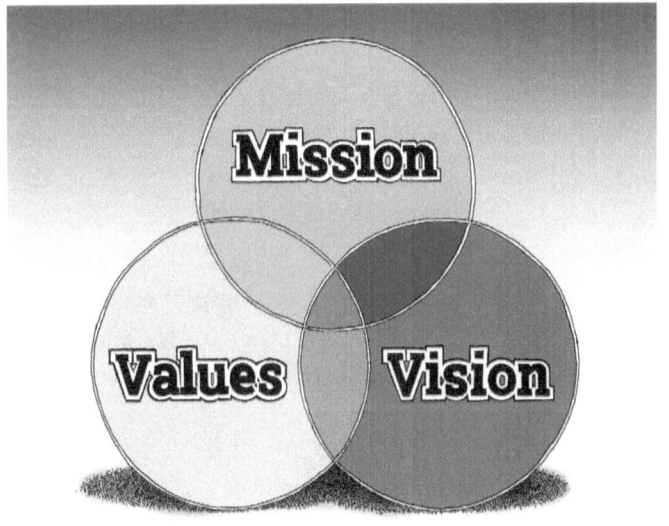

ONE OF THE FIRST THINGS A COMPANY SHOULD do is to develop a mission statement. People often confuse a mission statement with a vision statement. A vision statement sets the future goals of a company, while the mission statement guides how these goals will be achieved—the strategic decision-making. The mission statement tells the company's reason for existing.

Your company's mission statement should reflect your company's values, attitudes, and beliefs, which should reflect your personal values, attitudes, and beliefs. To help you develop your mission statement, you should answer the following questions:

- What is our business?

- Why do we exist?

- What are we trying to accomplish?

Having a mission statement will give your employees (and people who you deal with outside the organization) common goals. It will help guide employees in how to perform their jobs, how to treat customers, and how to represent the company. Without a mission statement, you may find that your employees will begin to operate by their own personal attitudes and beliefs, which may not be the same as yours.

Whether we realize it or not, we all have our own personal mission statements.

The length of the mission statement will vary from company to company, but the general rule is that it should be long enough to convey the message of the company. Generally, the best mission statements are no longer than two to three sentences. This way it's short enough for employees and even customers to remember.

Remember, your employees are representing you to your customers; you want to have a mission statement to guide their behavior.

"AN ORGANIZATION'S
ABILITY TO LEARN,
AND TRANSLATE THAT
LEARNING INTO ACTION
RAPIDLY, IS THE ULTIMATE
COMPETITIVE ADVANTAGE."

Jack Welch,
former Chairman and CEO of General Electric

LESSON 6:

THE BEST-RUN BUSINESSES HAVE LEADERS WHO UNDERSTAND THE LANGUAGES USED WITHIN THE ORGANIZATION.

I WAS WORKING IN A BUSINESS THAT WAS HAVING efficiency challenges, I requested the managers of the various departments meet to discuss potential solutions. We had people from finance, production, sales, customer service, human resources, and the service department in a room, and the boss began the meeting by defining our goals and asking for their full participation.

I come into a business without emotional connections and without a silver bullet or magic wand; the solutions are most often found within the business, offered up by the organization's employees.

It did not take long before the boss and I noticed many of the managers did not understand their peers. I studied the situation briefly and realized that each department was speaking a different language. The finance manager using "accounting speak," production was using words that the human resource manager did not understand. The customer service manager and the sales manager thought they knew what each other were trying to explain, but after the exchange of several questions, they soon realized they were not on the same page. The service manager was not talking at all, and when asked why not, he said he didn't understand what was being said so he just didn't say anything. He shut down and decided not to contribute to the conversation.

All the people in the room were stakeholders in the organization and each were chosen because they were the subject matter experts in their departments. The boss and I realized that we needed everyone to participate in order to solve our problems.

I called a "time out" and we discussed the communication challenge we were experiencing. The conclusion was this organization had a "literacy" problem. The managers knew the specific language of their departments, but they did not know enough of the languages used by the managers outside their field of expertise. Now I don't claim every manager needs to be an expert in all languages of the organization, but I do believe each manager has to be good enough at understanding most of the terms and meanings spoken in other departments in the organization. Think of it as knowing a "command language" for each department. This improved communication in the business would help to improve the efficiencies of the organization.

After talking with the boss, our solution was to develop a workshop and offer literacy training so each department manager and their key employees understood enough of the common languages, terms, and definitions used in the organization to be effective leaders. Now the rank-and-file employee may not need to understand the language of the financials, for example, but the managers of all departments would need to be literate in the common terms found on the financial statements, especially the profit and loss statement.

For example, if you have financial literacy you can participate in and contribute to the financial conversations. If you do not have financial literacy, the people in the conversation will tend to dumb down the conversation or exclude you altogether. You may be able to lead people, but how can you reach your full potential if you do not understand the financial statement you are responsible for as a leader?

Communication begins with understanding the language. Understanding the language is critical to identifying the problem, developing a plan, implementing solutions, and eventually analyzing the results. As the boss, you are responsible for the literacy of your organization. Help your leaders reach their full potential by improving the literacy in your organization, ultimately improving your profitability.

MANAGEMENT SKILLS

"PULL THE STRING AND IT WILL FOLLOW WHEREVER YOU WISH. PUSH IT, AND IT WILL GO NOWHERE AT ALL."

Dwight D. Eisenhower,
34th President of the United States of America

LESSON 1:

HAVE YOU OR DO YOU KNOW OF SOMEONE WHO HAS BEEN AFFLICTED BY THE CABBAGE MOTH SYNDROME?

T HIS LESSON WAS TAUGHT TO ME BY MY OLDEST grandson a few years ago. One Easter Sunday, my daughter planned an Easter egg hunt for my grandson. She placed tiny miniature marshmallows into a dozen or so brightly colored plastic Easter eggs and placed them in the yard in plain sight and in a row. She then pointed them out to my grandson, who immediately went to the nearest one and opened it. He was excited to see the miniature marshmallows inside and promptly ate them. He then went to the next nearest egg and opened it, thrilled to find more marshmallows. All the time this was going on my daughter was recording him on her iPhone. She was planning to share the video with friends and family on Facebook.

Everything was going great until this cabbage moth showed up. This tiny white moth flew in front of my grandson, distracted him, and led him off in another direction. Obviously this frustrated my daughter, who was busy filming. She became noticeably agitated with the boy. I suggested she be patient and wait a few minutes. My grandson, who was easily distracted, knew where the next colored egg was and I assured my daughter that he would be back. In a minute or so the cabbage moth flew away and the boy came back to almost the exact spot he left to pick up and open the remaining colored eggs, eating the treats inside.

If you have a tendency to be afflicted with the "Cabbage Moth Syndrome," know how it affects others on your team, especially if you are the boss. If you are around someone who is often afflicted, know that they will usually reengage after the distraction has dissipated. We can control our own behavior; we can only hope to influence the behavior of others. As a leader in your organization, do you understand how your actions affect others on your team?

"TREAT EMPLOYEES LIKE
THEY MAKE A DIFFERENCE,
AND THEY WILL."

Jim Goodnight,
CEO of SAS Institute

LESSON 2:
HOW DO YOU BUILD LOYALTY IN YOUR ORGANIZATION?

ONE MORNING JAKE CAME INTO MY OFFICE. He sat down and with a serious look on his face said, "Gary, you're going to have to fire me." Of course I asked, "Why?" We had just purchased the company, and when you do that you get the good, the bad, and the ugly of the old company. Jake was definitely part of the good. He was a certified welder, trained in the military, and a genuine, nice guy.

He said that he would not be able to pass the drug test. We did pre-employment drug testing but did not do it for employees who came into our company through acquisition. We did do random drug testing and Jake was certain when his number came up he would not pass. I asked him, "Do you want to leave the company?" He emphatically said no, but what were his choices? He knew that everyone was subject to the random drug testing, even the owners, so he was certain we would not make exceptions. He was right.

But in my mind we did have some options if Jake was willing to comply with certain rules. We began to discuss our Employee Assistance Program (EAP). His old company did not have such a program and he was not familiar with it. I said if he would agree to enroll in the program and actively participate in the treatment they would recommend, I would keep him on. The minute he failed to comply he would be gone. Jake agreed.

I adjusted his work schedule so he would have time to go to treatment, we adjusted his work duties so he did not handle any heavy equipment, and we agreed that this would be kept confidential to the other employees. I did tell my partner, who could not believe I did not fire him on the spot. I assured him that, "I got this" and it wouldn't affect him in the least. I said, "Let's see where this goes."

All in all, Jake got clean, stayed on with our company, participated in the random drug testing, and became one of the "leaders without stripes" on our manufacturing floor. Anytime an employee would begin to complain about little things they felt were unfair or didn't like, Jake would step in and set them straight. He even brought his brother into the company, another talented welder, and others he recruited to join our company.

At the end of the day, if I had fired Jake I would not have been able to help him help himself. What were we about really? Were we just another company that made stuff or were we a group of people who took care of each other and eventually became somewhat of a family? We became an employer of choice and a great place to work for those raising a family. Take care of your people first, profits will follow.

"IN MOST CASES, BEING
A GOOD BOSS MEANS
HIRING TALENTED PEOPLE
AND THEN GETTING
OUT OF THE WAY."

Tina Fey,
Actress, Comedian, Producer, and Playwright

LESSON 3:
DOES IT MATTER HOW THE TOWELS ARE FOLDED?

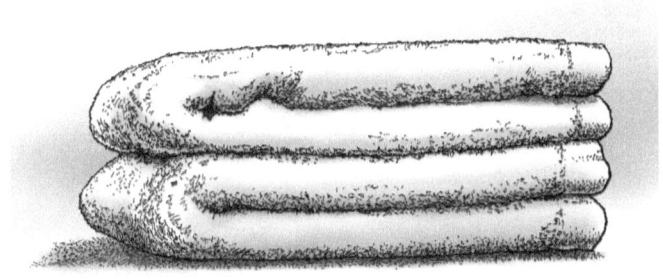

ONCE IN A WHILE I GET A CHANCE TO RIDE along with a project manager or foreman to visit a job site. This gets me out of the client's office and onto a job site, but more importantly it allows me time to talk with employees in a neutral environment, usually a pickup truck.

On my last ride-along I heard about a business owner who was a micromanager. He set the policies and procedures for all areas of his company. Now he has every right to do so, but at times it could be counterproductive.

In this situation I asked the employee how he would change a procedure to improve a problem area we were discussing. He gave me a comprehensive outline that seemed to have a lot of merit and could improve efficiencies. I asked if he suggested it to the boss. He just smiled at me and said, "When was the last time you remember the boss changing his mind?" Well I thought about it and he did have a point. The boss didn't change his mind often—seldom if ever. I thought about this ride and the lessons the employee taught me that day.

If the boss seldom, if ever, changes his mind, why would an employee contribute their good ideas to the cause? This business owner was a micromanager and wanted each task done exactly the way he felt it should be done.

This reminded me of when I was a young boy and lived at home with my five sisters (it's okay to feel sorry for me). One of my tasks was to fold the dish towels after they had been washed. I was told exactly how to fold them and every towel was to be folded the same way, no exceptions! I folded them as perfectly as I could, and to this day I can still fold dish towels exactly how I was taught as a young boy.

Today in our household we share the chores, and one such chore is folding towels, which is an individual task. I fold the towels one way; my wife folds them another way, and our children fold them their way. It is more important that the towels get folded than exactly how they are to be folded. It makes it easier for all of us to participate in the household chores, and the job gets done.

In essence the boss wants each employee to do their job exactly how he wants it done, regardless of whether the employee could improve on the process. This type of management style will stifle innovation in the workplace. If an employee has a better way, why wouldn't the boss welcome suggestions on how to improve the efficiencies of a specific process?

Giving employees the option to improve the process and do their jobs better can benefit everyone. Of course there are some sensitive jobs that need Standard Operating Procedures (SOPs) and should be done exactly the same way each time, but not all jobs need this type of structure.

Innovative employees are hard to come by and have the option to move on to other opportunities if not appreciated and valued. Having a culture of open communication will facilitate this type of innovative culture; allowing employees to take mitigated risks, celebrating their successes, and helping them learn from the shortfalls of their decisions will benefit the organization in the long run.

Smart business owners tap into their innovative employees and benefit from their fresh and new ideas. Innovation cannot happen if every employee is told exactly how to fold the towel, no exceptions! Innovation begins with freedom to think for oneself. Allow your employees to think for themselves and they will join you in contributing to the success of your business.

"I HATED EVERY MINUTE OF TRAINING, BUT I SAID, 'DON'T QUIT. SUFFER NOW AND LIVE THE REST OF YOUR LIFE AS A CHAMPION.'"

Muhammad Ali,
American Professional Boxer, and Activist

LESSON 4:
IF IT'S NOT WRONG, IT MUST BE RIGHT, RIGHT?

A S A BUSINESS CONSULTANT I'VE BEEN PRIVI-leged to work with business owners who wanted to improve their operations and increase their bottom-line results. During this process I get to know their businesses intimately and in doing so we often uncover inefficiencies and sometimes errors in tasks performed by employees who are doing what they feel is the right thing.

Once these errors are uncovered, the boss often wants to react quickly with disciplinary actions or other penalties they feel are appropriate for the mistake. I caution them to first look in the mirror with regards to their own missteps. When I talk with the employee(s) who have been doing these tasks, they often explain that they didn't fully understand their job because of a poor onboarding process and/or poor training practices. They tell me they really were not sure if what they were doing was correct and the boss was often not around to ask. This will happen in smaller companies where the boss wears several hats and is often on the move to get things done.

The employee will say they did what they felt was best and then they wait! They wait for the boss to react to their work and if nothing happens, they feel "it must be right." What happens afterward compounds the issue. Because the boss didn't give them feedback on the task, the employee sees the process as being done correctly, and as a result they have established their own Individual Operating Procedure (IOP) for that task. When we discover these errors and the boss realizes that almost every employee has established their own IOPs for their specific job tasks, again the boss is quick to get upset with their employees. Is this the right response?

Because the boss did not carve out the appropriate time to work on their business, these types of situations occur, often resulting in lost efficiencies and profits. The majority of the fault lies with the boss, who did not set Standard Operating Procedures (SOPs) in place to avoid many of these types of errors.

With SOPs in place, employees would not have to guess at what is correct, they would know. SOPs are especially important if the organization does not have a strong training process in place. Employees look for structure and training, in most cases they will be happy to do the task right, once they know what right is.

Better communications, time carved out to work on the business, and setting in place SOPs for important tasks (if not all tasks) will cure most of these shortcomings and produce a better culture within your organizations. Look in the mirror before you react, it may save you time and money.

"YOUR MOST UNHAPPY
CUSTOMERS ARE YOUR
GREATEST SOURCE
OF LEARNING."

Bill Gates,
Co-Founder of Microsoft and Philanthropist

LESSON 5:
WHAT'S A CUSTOMER WORTH? IF YOU ROLL THE DICE, YOU COULD "CRAP OUT!"

IN A RECENT MANAGERS MEETING I ATTENDED, there was a discussion regarding a poorly performing employee who was disrupting coworkers and exemplifying very poor customer service. The boss's initial knee-jerk reaction was to say, "Fire her!" The employee's supervising manager lobbied the boss to keep her on duty until he could hire a replacement to take her place.

This was a service business already operating in an understaffed position due to a low unemployment environment and lack of qualified applicants. A position that most employers are experiencing in today's economy. As I listened to the discussion, I began to hear the boss's position change as he was being sawed by the supervising manager.

After a while I began to ask a few questions to get their attention. What does it cost to lose a customer? How hard is it to gain a new customer? We already know how challenging it is to find good workers in today's world. I continued, in my experience when a company retains a bad employee, it is hard for the very good employees to justify staying with the company.

The good employees leave not because they cannot do the job; they leave because they do not feel comfortable in the company culture. They know how hard they work compared to others, they are confident in their abilities and feel they will be successful wherever they work. They may have already been contacted by your competition because when you are in a very low unemployment market, "The good employees leave because they can, and the poor employees stay because they have no choice!" If you keep poorly performing employees on staff simply because you need a "warm body," you are jeopardizing your established relationships with your customers and the culture of your organization.

I fully understand the impulse of not wanting to fire an employee until you have a replacement, but at what expense? The boss and I stayed and continued our conversation in private where I said, "I'd rather close down temporarily for a day or close early one day a week until a new recruit can be hired than keep a poor employee solely to fill a shift." The boss stated what he estimated the lost income would be to close an hour early, or worse, a day a week. I asked how that compared to a lost customer's annual spend or the onboarding and training expense of a new replacement when a very good employee leaves for a better culture.

At the end of our conversation we agreed to disagree. The poorly performing employee kept her job and filled a shift, the supervising manager kept looking for her replacement between the damage control he had to do to keep other employees from walking out, and the company continued to roll the dice and hope they didn't lose customers or employees due to their decision.

As I taught about this exchange, I realized that the issue of poor customer service was not the real issue after all. Poor customer service was a result of poor management who tolerated poor customer service, poor management was a result of the boss allowing management to keep employees on staff that gave poor customer service. What was the real issue? I would say it is the boss creating a culture that valued a warm body over great customer service. I don't know about you, but I have worked too hard and risked too much to roll the dice with the success of my business. I consider this type of management a crapshoot!

"HAVING A GREAT WORK CULTURE IS NOT AN OPTION – IT IS A NECESSITY."

Vani Kola,
Founder & Managing Director of Kalaari Capital

LESSON 6
EMPLOYEE RETENTION DOESN'T HAVE TO BE A BIG PROBLEM!

D ID YOU KNOW THAT IN TODAY'S WORKFORCE we have four to five generations of workers? This made me think of the businesses I know that truly understand how to manage the various challenges that come with a diverse workforce. I get into many organizations and have the privilege to talk with many business owners on a daily and weekly basis. In recent discussions with some organizations, I hear their main concern is retaining the employees they have and stopping the employee turnover they are experiencing. From other organizations this topic does not come up unless I bring it up. I was curious why some businesses have huge retention issues and others do not.

In my opinion there are many reasons for this. One overarching reason for poor retention is the boss's lack of understanding of the several generations in their present-day workforce. Here are a few points to think about.

First, I have been carrying an AARP card in my wallet for more than a decade now. In my generation I was trained in an autocratic management style. If you didn't like what the boss said and didn't comply with the boss's demands, you would often hear, "My way or the highway!" There was no discussion and you were expected to do what you were told. As many of us know too well this is not the case today, and in my opinion, we are all better off because of it. Bottom line: the boss cannot manage like they were managed years ago! The boss must change with the times.

Second, I feel managers of my generation do understand the employees we have that are the ages of our children. My children are in their late thirties and early forties, and I feel I have a handle on what motivates them and how to manage this segment of the workforce because I was there as this generation grew up. This generation must be the bridge between the boss and the younger generations of our workforce. They can give valuable input into establishing and managing a diverse culture.

Third, as I think about retention in today's economy, I see the organizations that have little to no retention problems are the companies that have a culture that supports the lifestyles of the various generations. Some of the younger employees we have are not necessarily working for a certain hourly wage but are working for a certain lifestyle. That lifestyle may include working from home a few days a week, it may be working at various jobs within the organization (becoming cross-trained) to keep from becoming bored with their main jobs, and it may include more single days off rather than the week's vacation we grew up with. These are just a few observations I have noticed as I talk with various managers and the boss, and I am sure you can add a few more from your organization.

Culture begins with the boss and filters down throughout the organization. The boss cannot create a culture that he or she grew up in. Today is a very different world. I often address myself as the old white guy in the room. As that old white guy, I must listen and learn from the younger generations as to what motivates them and what they see as their career tracks. What I have found is their understanding of a career is much different than what I had as a career. The organizations that understand this and create cultures that nurture an environment that welcomes diverse generations are the organizations that do not have runaway retention rates and ultimately have a healthier bottom line.

"TELL ME AND I FORGET.
TEACH ME AND I REMEMBER.
INVOLVE ME AND I LEARN."

Benjamin Franklin,
Founding Father of the U.S.

LESSON 7:
BUSINESS OWNER AS TEACHER AND COACH.

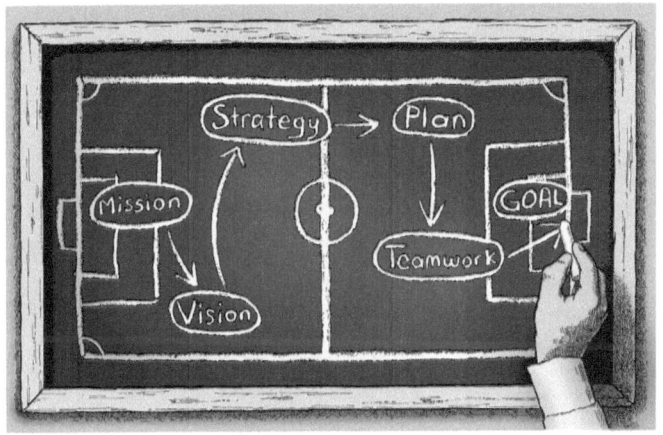

I WAS REVIEWING THE MONTHLY FINANCIALS with the boss in advance of sending them to his banker; one of the services I offer is coaching the boss how to manage a banking relationship. I was challenging the boss with a few questions regarding the change in his backlog. The backlog for the previous month was close to a million dollars and now for this month it was next to nothing, and the revenues did not reflect the million dollars in sales.

We took a step back to analyze why and search out the root cause of the misinformation. Come to find out the production manager, who was only a few months out of the field and now in a management position, had made an error when estimating the backlog.

It didn't take long to determine that the production manager was never taught how to calculate the backlog. Fortunately, in this case we caught the error and adjusted the information prior to sending the financials to the boss's bank. After we found the problem the boss and I had a few conversations about how to fix the situation so it did not reoccur.

What I explained to the boss, who was a hard-driving no-nonsense manager, was that one of his main duties as owner of the company was to teach! This is something the boss knew in the back of his mind but never invested a lot of energy or time in, especially with his young inexperienced managers. The good thing about this problem was the young manager was totally dedicated to the company and was eager to learn. He understood he needed more training and was looking forward to the one-on-one time with the boss.

Remember when you were in school and your full-time job was to be a student? Your teachers were the subject matter experts and your job was to learn the lessons. These young managers are not that far removed from school and still have that mindset. They are open to learning from the boss, the company's subject matter expert. Spend time with these young people and offer the benefits of your years of wisdom. You may experience a lot of personal satisfaction as you pass along the fine points of the job and coach them to their peak performance.

If the boss does not teach the new managers they will either get the information from others in the organization, and the information may or may not be accurate—not accurate in this case—or with these younger managers you can expect they will Google their questions and think whatever comes up on Google is the correct answer. Neither of these scenarios are what you want for your company.

The boss explained to me that he had tons of work and the teaching and coaching thing was not necessarily in his character. I explained that these young managers would get the information one way or the other, and would he want to control the process or have others steer the ship?

Teaching and coaching others is as important as knowing when to work on your business and when to work in your business. It is a learned discipline and the boss will have to decide how important it is to his company and dedicate his time and talents to developing the next generation of managers.

"START WITH GOOD PEOPLE,
LAY OUT THE RULES,
COMMUNICATE WITH YOUR
EMPLOYEES, MOTIVATE
THEN AND REWARD THEM."

Lee Iacoca,
former President, and Chairman of Chrysler Corp.

LESSON 8:
WHERE IS THE BEST PLACE TO RECRUIT GOOD EMPLOYEES?

MY SON WAS PLAYING BASKETBALL IN OUR driveway one summer day and my wife made the comment that his friends were so nice and courteous. I assured her that our son was just as nice and courteous as those other boys. How did I know this? Watch your kids' friends when they come to your house to spend time with your son or daughter. I would notice how our kids' friends would act, the words they would use, if they played fair and were courteous. I believe this is how our son or daughter behaved when they visited their friends' houses.

I told my wife I believe that when our kids host friends at our house, our kids are on their best behavior because we are there, and they know we are watching what is happening. Their friends aren't as worried about what we think because we are not their parents. When our kids went to their friends' houses, I am sure they would act as their friends do at our house. Why do I think this? Because we hang out with people we like. We choose our friends because we have things in common and share many of the same values and beliefs. That's why we choose them as friends!

Do the same with your current employees. Notice their work habits. How do they dress and talk when they are at work? Do they show up for their shifts? Do they make fewer mistakes than other employees? I'm sure you can add a lot more traits to this list. Employees who have these types of positive traits are employees we would like to clone. These are the employees we should be asking, "Do you have a friend or two who would like to work for our company?"

Let the best employees know that they are your best employees. Ask them why they enjoy their jobs. My contention is they do, that is one reason they are some of your best employees to start with. People enjoy working with people they like. Think about it, mining your future workforce from recommendations your top employees suggest just makes good business sense.

I think one of the best places to find good employees starts in your organization. Be proactive and let your top employees know that you want more employees like them. Some owners would push back on this recommendation, saying, "If I tell them they are my best employees then they will want more money!" Well yeah! I would suggest paying your top performers a higher wage because they are worth more to your organization. Likewise, I would pay underperforming employees less because they are not as efficient and could even be considered a liability to your organization.

Your best people know they are the best and they know they are worth more than the person next to them. Don't think they haven't thought of this and they are still with you. Why? Because wages are not the main reason people stay with an organization. It's about people. If they like you as the boss and you treat them with dignity and respect, they will stay with your organization because they feel valued. If you don't believe me, I would suggest you ask them.

I have found when I begin working in an organization and I ask people if they feel valued, most people are honest with me and say what they really feel. I can find out in short order if the boss is a great person to work for or someone they really don't trust, because they will tell me so.

Be the boss that you would like to work for and ask your top performers to recruit their friends to join your great organization. It's convenient, inexpensive, and above all, it creates results.

"YOU DON'T BUILD A BUSINESS. YOU BUILD PEOPLE, THEN PEOPLE BUILD THE BUSINESS."

Zig Ziglar,
American Author and Motivational Speaker

LESSON 9:
THE BOSS SHOULD BE THE TOP CHEERLEADER IN THE ORGANIZATION!

I HAVE BEEN A RUNNER FOR MANY YEARS. I BEGAN running in high school when I joined the cross-country team where our coach was Coach Jensen. I tried to remember his full name for this chapter, but I was unable to do so because for years he was just Coach Jensen.

I remember when we first started running with Coach Jensen, he told all the freshmen if we would bend our thumbs into our palms and wrap our fingers around our thumbs, holding the thumbs tight when we ran, that we could run faster. So all the guys on our team would be holding our thumbs when we ran.

We would run every day after school and Coach Jensen would lead the pack. Every so often one of us would lag behind the group and Coach Jensen would drop back and run with that person, encouraging him and cheering him on until he caught up to the pack, and then Coach Jensen would run ahead and lead the team once again.

I remember looking at our competition when we ran a meet and none of them were holding their thumbs the right way, which meant we had the advantage! Now I don't know if what Coach Jensen said was true about holding our thumbs a certain way to help us run faster, but I do know that each of us ran as hard as we could during our meets because Coach Jensen wanted us to and we didn't want to disappoint him. We ran for the other guys on the team because total points mattered in the meet and we didn't want to let the other guys down, and finally we ran for ourselves, which really was third on the list behind Coach and the guys. Why did we feel this way? I believe it was because of Coach Jensen's leadership.

I have been in business or consulting with the boss through the economic downturn of 2008, through the economic uncertainty of 9/11, and through the economic and healthcare crisis of COVID-19. What I saw from the best leaders during these challenging times was Coach Jensen's management style.

During normal business times the boss should exhibit this type of management style, and especially during challenging economic times the boss should develop relationships with the employees so individuals step up when the situation requires it purely because they don't want to disappoint the boss.

The boss should coach all the employees during challenging times but especially the employees who lag behind for whatever reason. It could be something outside of work or past experiences they had at other employers—the boss may not know why they struggle more than others on the team. But the boss should spend a little more time coaching these folks to be sure they don't fall so far behind the pack that they get lost and self-select off the team.

And finally, the boss should be the cheerleader for the organization, setting the mood and staying as positive as possible without delivering false hope to the organization. The personality of the organization reflects the personality of the boss. If the boss walks around saying the sky is falling, eventually people will believe the sky is falling; if the boss walks around saying we are a great team and we got this, the organization has a reason to believe they can weather the storm and come out whole on the other end.

The boss also needs to be sure everyone in the organization understands the competitive advantage the business has over the competition. Understanding there is an advantage can lower the stress of the staff, knowing the company has an upper hand in the market.

As the boss, be that great leader your team needs, be that motivational coach who encourages the team, and be that cheerleader giving the organization a reason to fight. Maybe even teach the employees the secret thumb trick. Who knows, it may be the advantage your team needs to win!

"GIVE ME SIX HOURS
TO CHOP DOWN A TREE
AND I WILL SPEND THE
FIRST FOUR HOURS
SHARPENING THE AXE."

Abraham Lincoln,
16th President of the United States of America

LESSON 10:
HEY BOSS, DISENGAGE AND RELAX!

I HAVE TO SAY UP FRONT THAT THIS CHAPTER IS one of those, "Do as I say and not what I have done most of my career!" chapters. When business is good the boss is most always in a good mood, and it's good to have him around. But when times are tuff, the boss can be a real pain!

I had a client who owned a specialty machine shop that made custom machine parts on demand. The boss #1 was the founder of the company and was transitioning the business to his son, the boss #2. My job was to coach the boss #2 through the transition until the boss #1 was convinced his son could run the place.

Now the only thing more frustrating than having one boss is having two bosses, especially for employees who are trying their best to do their jobs in stressful times. So coaching the employees through the transition was an added responsibility I did for the business's sake.

The transition went as smoothly as you could imagine, and afterward the boss #1 did retire...sort of—the most a founder can retire, which means he only visited a few hours a week to see what was happening. The son became the boss and we worked together for some time.

One issue the business had was 50% of their business was with one large customer who used this company exclusively for their custom machine parts. Later that year, the large customer was bought out by a competitor and the new owners decided to use several custom machine shops for parts. The result was the boss lost about 45% of his business within a few months. A great reason to diversify your customer base

As the revenue began to decrease the boss's stress began to increase. I would ask the boss on Monday what he did over the weekend, and he would reply, "I worked the whole weekend!" This lifestyle began to drain the business and especially the employees. I tried to explain to the boss that disengaging and relaxing was essential for him to be the best boss he could be.

I remember years ago when I was a young business owner, I did the same thing, and lucky for me, I had help at home. If you've read the previous chapters in this book, you might remember me saying that my wife is my best advisor, I just don't listen to her as much as

I should. When I was working too much, being a pain at home and work and super stressed out, she used to look at me and in her best "chairwoman of the board" voice she would say, "You need to go work out!" I appreciated the advice (okay, it was really an order) and I would go and run or take a long hike and clear my mind. I learned that this time away was very valuable for me and I do it today without being told. You see, I really am a lifelong learner.

As the boss you should learn to disengage your mind from the pressures of today so you can see past the trees into the forest. I used to feel the business closing in on me like being wrapped in a blanket from head to toe. You can image how smothering that would feel to the boss. This situation is not healthy for the boss, the boss's loved ones at home, the employees, and ultimately the business. If you think about it, it is damaging to everything the boss is working so hard for. Step back and disengage, this will allow you to truly relax. You will come back to work refreshed and rejuvenated.

I would highly recommend that you listen to your chairwoman or chairman of your board when they say, "You need to go work out!" Some of our most valuable advisors are the people who know us the best and the people we cannot bullshit. Be that lifelong learner and enjoy life to the fullest!

"DON'T FOLLOW THE CROWD. LET THE CROWD FOLLOW YOU."

Margaret Thatcher,
former Prime Minister of The United Kingdom

LESSON 11:
WHAT WAS THE BOSS THINKING? A LOOK INSIDE THE BOSS'S HEAD...

IF YOU DO NOT POSSESS AN ENTREPRENEURIAL mindset, the boss's decision-making process may look very risky to you. To the boss it makes perfect sense. Let me try to explain.

The boss receives a small piece of information. Most folks in the company see it as nonessential data with little meaning. The boss gets excited about the opportunity she sees and begins discussions to react to and move forward with a plan using the newly discovered information. The managers declare the data they have is at best only 25% of what they would need to even think about diverting resources and investing company funds. Well, the boss is "the boss" and a plan is developed, and the company begins to implement the plan.

In short order another 25% of the data is received, making the entire data collected 50% of what others would say is needed to begin thinking about developing a plan. The boss reviews the new information, and now with 50% of the data, she pivots and changes course. Still moving forward, she begins working the newly revised plan.

A short time passes and an additional 25% of the data is collected, so now the boss has 75% of the data collected, which is still short of what the managers feel would be needed to begin developing a plan. Adding to the 75% of data collected from the market, the boss and the managers have the information collected from the company's activities as it moves forward from the initial 25% to now 75% of the data.

At this point after reviewing the new data, the boss is willing to make a "go/no-go" decision. The boss and the managers must decide if this is a good investment of time and money or not. If not, the project is dropped for now. The managers may feel this whole ordeal was a waste of time, but the boss shrugs it off and looks for the next exciting project. If the data looks good, the company again pivots and changes course, and this time the managers begin to believe in the opportunity and the company is moving forward full throttle with the revised plan. The knowledge or intel the company has is very valuable and will differentiate the boss's company from the competition.

Today the entire market has 100% of the data and the opportunity is apparent. The competition is beginning to ramp up its resources to begin the process of developing a plan. The boss's company is light-years ahead of the competition, granted the risk was high that the data would result in a business opportunity back when the boss knew 25% of what she knows now, but the reward would also be high if the plan worked as the boss hoped it would. The company is ready to reap the rewards of early adoption in the market.

What magical sense does the boss have that gave her the confidence to move forward with only 25% of the data? This magical sense or feeling is called intuition. It is the gut feeling entrepreneurs have that tells them to jump before anyone even knows the opportunity exists. If you do not have this intuition or gut feeling, working for or with this type of personality can be nerve-racking and sometimes outright scary. But in my experiences, I have learned not to discard the boss's intuition, as it is often the difference between a business surviving or becoming one of the SBA's statistics.

If you do not have it, it is hard to understand. Your job is not to understand how the boss recognizes these unforeseen opportunities but to help her identify the ones that are too risky until the next 25% of data is received. I have often had to grab the boss from the ankles and pull her down to earth until the company received a little more data to move forward. Inside the boss's head it makes perfect sense, but from the company's point of view it looks to be very risky, mostly because it is!

"THE SINGLE BIGGEST
WAY TO IMPACT AN
ORGANIZATION IS TO
FOCUS ON LEADERSHIP
DEVELOPMENT."

John C. Maxwell,
American Author, and Speaker

LESSON 12:
AS THE BOSS, ARE YOU DEVELOPING LEADERS IN YOUR ORGANIZATION?

RECENTLY I HAVE BEEN IN SEVERAL DISCUS-sions with business owners revolving around leadership. In general, we have concluded that most organizations are experiencing inefficiencies in production, a disproportionate amount of waste, uncontrolled employee turnover, or many other issues that are a result of poor leadership skills. In most of these discussions the boss agrees that in their organizations they have very good workers, good to adequate managers, but they are lacking leaders.

The question is often raised, "Are people born leaders?" If so then business owners must identify and hire born leaders if they want to improve leadership in their organization. As the conversations mature, I often see the boss begin to think that some people are born to lead and have the natural talent to lead. This is different from being a born leader. What I see are talented employees in a growing organization, where the boss identifies them as a leader, and therefore that person is promoted and expected to lead.

Often these people are great workers, very good managers, and then promoted into a leadership position in which they underwhelm the boss. Why does this happen? Did the boss make a poor decision by promoting this person? I would contend they did not, but what the boss did not do was develop or train the new leader. Talent without training will most often underwhelm the boss and cause more problems in an organization.

What are some of the signals the boss needs to be aware of to identify poor leadership? The boss may hear, "Just tell them (employees) that I am their boss so they will do what I say!" or "I told them (employees) that already and they still haven't completed the work, so it's not my fault!" Obviously, these examples are coaching opportunities for the boss, but how do you stop these types of issues in your organization? Look for the root cause of the issue.

As you look for the root cause in your organization, here are a few examples to keep in mind.

The new leader wants to be or is friends with the staff and wants to remain friends as they assume the leadership role. As the boss you will need to emphasize respect first, friendship second. If the employees do not respect the leader, the leader will not be able to lead. This is an important lesson for first-time leaders as they develop their leadership style. Now in my opinion, I do not mean never be friends with the staff, but there needs to be a professional separation for the leader to be effective.

Second if the leader is insecure in their leadership abilities, they will resort to a micromanaging style of leadership. The insecure leader will try to control the situation by inserting themselves in a process that would ordinarily be done by a subordinate because they do not want the boss to think they did not lead the process.

An example of this would be the insecure leader sitting in on an initial interview, which would normally be done by a human resource person and/or an immediate supervisor. The leader does not trust that the employees can do as good a job as the leader can, so the leader hovers over the process, causing dissension and mistrust by the employees responsible for the hiring process.

Poor leadership can be a silent killer of your culture. Micromanaging cultivates mistrust, and as a result, fosters poor communication. The boss can derail this process by coaching the new leaders in their organization. As the boss your goal should be to develop your leaders to be smarter than you are when they get to be your age and occupy your position in an organization!

MARKETING STRATEGIES

"DIFFERENTIATE WITH VALUE OR DIE WITH PRICE."

Jeffery Gitomer,
American Author, Speaker, and Business Trainer

LESSON 1:
LOWER PRICES ARE NOT ALWAYS THE ANSWER!

O NE OF MY FIRST "OFFICIAL" JOBS I HELD, NOT counting the paper route that I had for years, was a clerk at a local grocery store. One of my first memories of working in the local store was when the owner, Mr. Prellwitz, came to me with a roll of scotch tape and several rolls of new pennies. He told me to tape a penny, with Lincoln's head facing up, on each of the loaves of bread, which were on several racks lined up against the wall. So I did exactly what Mr. Prellwitz asked of me, but even as a sixteen-year-old high school kid I had to wonder why I was doing this.

When I was done and Mr. Prellwitz came to inspect my work, I asked him, "Why did you have me do this?" He said the other grocery store in town was running a promotion and giving bread away to everyone who shopped in their store that day, and he was going to "do him one better" and pay his customers a penny to take his bread! He said it with an aggressive tone and, as I remember, was rather proud of the idea. Still, I couldn't figure out why he would first of all give something away for free and second of all pay someone to take it.

Looking back at this example it seems counterintuitive that a business would do something like this. But businesses sell on price every day. And when you sell on price, someone or another business can always sell it cheaper, even to the point of paying customers to take it as Mr. Prellwitz did.

If you cannot sell on price then how do you compete in an aggressive market?

Ask yourself, "What differentiates your business from the competition?" It cannot be price as that is too easily replicated. It has to be something more real! One answer has to do with psychographics. What do I mean? Think of the retailer Abercrombie & Fitch, known as A&F.

When my son was living at home he needed a new pair of jeans. I gave him $50 and told him to go buy himself a new pair. I waited patiently for several weeks but no new jeans and no $50. One day he came home with new A&F jeans. I asked him why it took him this long to buy the jeans. He responded, "Dad, I had to save the $100 extra I needed to buy their jeans."

Why did he pay $150 for a pair of jeans from A&F rather than saving himself $100 and buying a $50 pair elsewhere? If you think about it, my son paid $50 for the jeans and $100 for the "feeling" of having A&F on his hips. Those feelings are self-esteem, self-confidence, acceptance, status, success, quality, and the feeling of being liberal. All of these are psychographic feelings, and the stores that sell $50 jeans cannot compete for the same customers in the same way A&F does. Price is not why their customers buy A&F jeans and it is hard to compete against them, even when your price is one-third that of Abercrombie & Fitch.

If we think about it, most of our important buying decisions are decided using psychographics rather than price. Price is not a differentiator; it is a feature of the product. Psychographics, the way your products make your customers feel, are a benefit to your customers, and customers buy benefits! Don't get caught up in a pricing war, discover the psychographic reasons your customers buy from you and promote those reasons for greater growth and profitability.

"CHANGE IS THE LAW OF LIFE AND THOSE WHO LOOK ONLY TO THE PAST OR PRESENT ARE CERTAIN TO MISS THE FUTURE."

John F. Kennedy,
35th President of the United States of America

LESSON 2:
CHANGE IS HARD FOR THIS OLD GUY, SO WHAT DID I DO? I DID MY RESEARCH.

RECENTLY, I HIRED A MARKETING FIRM TO work with my company, Guident Business Solution, LLC, because I thought I needed a subject matter expert to help me evaluate how I communicate the benefits of my company in today's dynamic business environment.

Even though I was the one who initiated the relationship with a very well-known professional company I had resisted making some of the changes they suggested. One such change was the redesign of my company logo, which I have had since 2009 when I started the company, and by the way, I designed the logo myself.

I don't know why I resisted, maybe because I designed it or because I invested significantly in promoting the logo in the market.

So what did I do? I went on a quest to prove that my logo was the better design, of course. After all, I am the business owner and I launched this company many years ago and just to be sure, we are doing very well helping businesses succeed and grow. Why change something that is not broken, I thought! So I began to ask the opinions of some of my most trusted advisors and others who did not know I existed prior to this point. Frankly, I would ask anyone who was in earshot!

As I began my research I would ask which of these two logos looks better? This unproven redesigned logo or this old and trusted logo? Now I don't remember asking the question in just that manner, but some of my most trusted and honest advisors suggested I was moving forward with a more than slight bias! I guess they may have been right. Nonetheless, repeatedly I received the unexpected response that the new logo was an improvement and of the two logos most (okay, all who I asked) said the new logo was the clear winner.

Today I am using the new logo and truth be told, I am very happy with the results. A more import lesson for me is the fact that I had to pivot and accept the advice of the subject matter expert I hired. As the owner of the business I get asked my opinion every day. I consider myself the subject matter expert in my business and I am very comfortable having others look to me for guidance. Having to step back and take advice and/ or direction is not my strong suit, so it is even more important for me to listen to those experts I have hired who are suggesting improvements to my business. As a person who has been running various businesses for more than forty years, this has been a valuable lesson learned.

I often think of the logo lesson when I suggest to business owners to create an advisory team for their business. I suggest these original advisory team members: your CPA, your banker, and your lawyer. Additional professionals can be consulted as needed, such as a professional marketing firm. This team is charged with advising the owner when important decisions need to be made. I often say, "I am much smarter in a room full of people than I am by myself."

Surrounding ourselves with smart employees and accomplished advisors is just good business. Best of luck creating your team of advisors!

"QUALITY IN A SERVICE OR
PRODUCT IS NOT WHAT
YOU PUT IN IT. IT IS WHAT
THE CLIENT OR CUSTOMER
GETS OUT OF IT."

Peter Drucker,
former Management Consultant and Educator

LESSON 3:
IF YOU SELL CHEVYS AND DELIVER CADILLACS, IT WILL COST YOU!

I MAGINE GOING TO YOUR LOCAL CAR DEALER AND ordering a brand-new Chevy. When you go back to the dealership to pick up your new car, the dealer insists that you take a Cadillac home with you at the Chevy price. This does not make sense and you can't imagine that it would ever happen this way, but I see this kind of thing happen in businesses more often than you would think. Why would the boss allow this?

The boss stresses high quality in everything the company does. Without proper direction from the boss employees may tend to sell Chevy quality and deliver Cadillac quality for the Chevy price. When I see this, I bring it to the attention of the boss and I may hear,

"Our company is driven on top quality, we advertise top quality, and we deliver top quality!"

I will begin the conversation by saying, "If the customer pays for Chevy quality, they are expecting to receive Chevy quality, and when you deliver Chevy quality, you have met the customer's expectation and you have done your job well. If the customer expects Chevy quality and your company delivers Cadillac quality for the Chevy quality price, your bottom line of the company will suffer, and the customer may not even appreciate the higher quality for the lower price."

How do you know this is happening and how do we correct this issue of lost profits in your organization?

I explain to the boss that this can be discovered during the job costing phase of the operations. After each job has been completed, doing an analysis of the costs verses the selling price of the job will uncover if the customer received a higher quality product than they paid for because the profit of the job will suffer.

Higher quality is not a bad thing if the customer pays a higher price for that higher quality product. We don't go into the Cadillac dealership and insist that we buy that Cadillac for the Chevy price. As consumers we are trained to pay a higher price for better quality. It works that way with everything we buy from our groceries to our new homes.

If the profitability of your company is lower than you feel it should be, as the boss it is your responsibility to find the problem. Begin by investigating a few jobs by checking the costs against the expected profitability of that job. If the profits are not there, you may discover that you are delivering a much higher quality than your customers are paying for or even expect.

As the boss you insist on high quality for your customers, obviously, and this is not a bad thing. As you train your staff, you must explain what you mean by high quality and meeting the customer's expectation. When you over deliver, the bottom line of your company suffers and the customer may not even realize they got a deal! As the boss you must define what high quality is for your organization and stress that when you meet your customer's expectations, you will have happy customers and have done your job well.

"RUNNING A BUSINESS WELL MEANS KNOWING WHEN IT'S TIME TO MAKE A PROFIT."

Auliq Ice,
Founder of Icetratt Foundation for Social Investments

LESSON 4:
BY THE NUMBERS: WHERE DO DISCOUNTS COME FROM, REVENUES OR PROFIT?

MANY OF MY CLIENTS HAVE SALES STAFF AND pay sales commission on top-line revenues. I often get the question regarding my opinion on offering a discount to close the deal. I usually give the boss a typical consultant's answer like, "It depends." I begin the discussion by asking the boss where the discount is coming from. They look at me with a somewhat puzzled look and ask, "What are you talking about?"

Most of the business owners I work with see discounts coming solely off of top-line revenues. For example, they may have a $10,000 proposal that is in a competitive situation, and their salesperson believes they need to discount the job in order to get the work. Together they may believe a $1,000 discount is necessary to close the deal. A 10% reduction in price to get the job and reach their revenue goals, keep their people working, and possibly steal a competitor's customer is acceptable in their minds. It very well may be, but we need to understand the full impact of the discount as it pertains to net profit, not just top-line revenues.

We continue the discussion and I ask, "What is the profit margin on the original proposal?" For this example let's say this proposal will generate a 40% gross profit or $4,000 ($10,000 × 40%), so that $1,000 discount, which was 10% of revenue is also 25% of gross profit ($1,000 ÷ $4,000). This 25% discount on gross profit may not be what the boss intended, but he may still think it's okay in order to get the job.

Taking this job a step further, let's say the proposal has a net profit of 15% after overhead is factored in. I factor overhead into every job. Why? Because every dollar of revenue has to pay for its part of the company's total overhead. By definition I am using overhead to include all expenses not captured in total cost of goods sold. In this example the company has a year-to-date overhead of 25% of revenues; this means that every $1 of revenue has to contribute 25¢ toward overhead. Think about this: where else does the company get the funds to pay for the overhead? Answer: from every dollar of revenue it generates.

So in our example the net profit from this proposal is estimated to be 15% (40% gross profit minus 25% overhead) of the $10,000 total proposal or a net profit on this job of $1,500 ($10,000 × 15%). Now take the discount as a percentage of the net profit and you are planning to reduce the net profit on this job by two-thirds ($1,500 net profit minus $1,000 discount leaving $500 of net profit). If you think about discounts as coming from the net profit of a job rather than off of the top-line revenue of a job, it puts it in a different light and may cause an owner to think twice before offering a discount, remembering that net profit is a major contributor to the owner's equity of the business.

One point I want to stress is that we are estimating (and eventually will be job costing after the job is completed) to a net profit number and not a gross profit number when we include overhead as part of the calculation.

What is the best-case scenario? In my opinion, selling on price alone is not a sustainable business model. Identifying your company's differentiators such as quality products, custom products, timeliness of delivery, industry relationships, etc. and training sales staff how to close deals using these competitive advantages will generate more profits in the long run and may keep your company out of a pricing war in your market.

The book *Blue Ocean Strategy* by W. Chan Kim and Renée A. Mauborgne is a good read that explains this concept in more detail. Your numbers may be larger or smaller and your percentages will vary, but the principle will remain constant. Discounts may be a necessary evil, and understanding discounts as a percentage of net profit rather than solely coming off of top-line revenues is necessary as we strive to grow owner's equity.

"THE KEY IS TO MAKE MISTAKES FASTER THAN THE COMPETITION, SO YOU HAVE MORE CHANCES TO LEARN AND WIN."

Tommy Hilfiger,
Founder of Tommy Hilfiger Corporation

LESSON 5:
WHAT IS YOUR COMPANY'S COMPETITIVE ADVANTAGE?

In my work I have often been approached with these questions: "Do you think this is a good idea?" and "Should I go into business?" I usually ask the questioners to further describe their business idea for me. They begin by speaking calmly and at an average pace, but as they begin to get excited, their vocal tone starts to rise, the pace of their speech increases, and they often become animated. This is a great sign since it shows they have a true passion for what they are describing. Passion for what you're doing is one of the critical ingredients for success as a small business owner.

Next, I ask them to describe their competitive advantage. If they respond with, "What's that?" I tell them not to quit their day job, end of discussion. Having and identifying a competitive advantage is so important that if a business owner cannot describe their competitive advantage, then I believe they are destined for failure.

As the owner of your business, you must identify or develop your company's competitive advantage. Once you've done that, you have to teach your key management and employees how you plan to use your competitive advantage to outsell the competition and increase your company's market share. In order to identify your competitive advantage, you should compare the advantages and disadvantages of your business against two or more competitors. Pay particular attention in the major areas of price, location, image, products/services, customer service, and quality.

Here is an example of a competitive advantage: each morning I stop at a local drive-through coffee shop where the coffee tastes good, is affordable, and has a convenient drive-through. I do this often enough that I would consider this *my* coffee shop and an important part of my morning routine. Now let's say you open a drive-through coffee shop directly across the street from *my* coffee shop. How are you going to get me to stop buying coffee at my favorite drive-through and instead spend my coffee allowance at your drive-through? If you are successful, whatever the reason, that reason is your competitive advantage. Identify it and communicate it to all who will listen.

"PROFIT IS NOT A CAUSE BUT A RESULT."

Peter Drucker,
former Management Consultant and Educator

LESSON 6:
DON'T LET THE BIG ONE (PROFIT) GET AWAY!

I WAS IN CANADA FISHING FOR MUSKIES WITH MY son, and we were using surface baits when I saw this huge V heading for my bait. I immediately became excited and, in an instant, could visualize a large trophy-size muskie hanging on my wall in the man cave. I watched the lure and asked my son to man the net, then in an instant, I pulled back the rod to set the hook—and nothing.

In my excitement I forgot everything I knew about the art of fishing and I set the hook before the fish bit the lure. I pulled the lure out of the water and my trophy catch was gone. It makes for a good story at the lodge, but I have nothing to show for my efforts.

In the past few weeks, I have seen this happen to more than one of my clients' businesses. The boss was working to land a huge account. He was getting excited and even planning what to do with the excess profits a large job like this could bring. The issue I saw in every case was the larger the job, the lower the profit margin.

The boss was timid and was not confident charging his regular rates when it came to the larger jobs. I understand better than most the benefit of cash flow from these larger jobs and in some unique circumstances, such as a seasonal business, landing a large job for the sake of cash flow is important. But giving up too much margin for the sake of landing a large job does not make good business sense.

The boss must have the confidence in himself and his team that if priced reasonably, his company will "land the big one." I often told my sales team their jobs were to get us in the door by selling our quality and follow-through so we had an opportunity to bid the work. My job was to price the work to achieve a win-win situation. If the only win was for the customer, then we did not do our jobs well enough. If the only win was in our favor, then again, we would have failed.

I don't ever want the big jobs to get away, but I am not eager to do the larger jobs for next to no profits. As the boss you must set the direction for your company and sell on quality and not price. It is easy for anyone to get excited or even mesmerized by the large numbers. This is when the boss should jump into teaching mode and educate the staff about the risks to profitability of the larger jobs. Experience will tell you to be cautious and proceed with care when estimating those jobs. An employee working on a commission basis will naturally get excited with the large numbers, but the boss understands the risks and rewards and must make the call.

Don't allow yourself to get so excited to win the big job or so afraid that you may lose the big job that you forget the lessons that got you where you are today. Land that big one and tell the tales of large profitable jobs, not those profits that got away!

CONCLUSION

I HAVE BEEN COLLECTING THESE REAL-LIFE STO-
ries my entire consulting career. Over the years, I
have worked with business owners, managers, and team
members to help identify and fix problems that challenge the boss or the management team. I have helped
with marketing, human resources, management issues,
company culture, strategic planning, and my specialty,
finances.

You might have picked out the most common issue
after reading this book, which is cash flow. But what is
the deeper issue beyond cash flow? That's what I have
had the pleasure of helping the boss discover.

I hope reading these short experiences have helped give
you some insight into any issue, large or small, that you
might be having within your own organization or team.
Thank you for reading about my real-life experiences in
business. If you want to continue reading new stories
every month, sign up for my monthly newsletter at:

garytvaughan.com/newsletter

GLOSSARY

Annual Operating Budget

A budget that lays out a company's projected income and expenses for a twelve-month period. It involves balancing out a business's sources of income against its expenses.

Balanced Scorecard

A strategic management performance metric used to identify and improve various internal business functions and their resulting external outcomes.

Balance Sheet

A financial statement that reports a company's assets, liabilities, and shareholders' equity at a specific point in time. It also provides a basis for computing rates of return and evaluating its capital structure.

Cabbage Moth Syndrome

When an employee is distracted by other projects and diverges from the initial project that the boss wants him or her to do.

Capital Investment
A sum of money provided to a company to further its business objectives.

Cash-Cowing
Pocketing the business's profits without reinvesting enough into capital expenditures to keep the organization going.

Cash Flow
The net amount of cash and cash equivalents being transferred into and out of a business.

Competitive Advantage
An advantage gained over other competitors by offering consumers greater value.

Controller
An individual who has responsibility for all accounting-related activities within a company, e.g., high-level account, managerial accounting, and financial services.

Corporatize
To subject to corporate ownership or control.

Employment-At-Will Statement
A statement that helps employees and non-employees understand that employment with the company is voluntary between both the company and the employee.

Employment Manual

Also known as employee handbook. The manual provides job-related information that is given to employees by their employer.

Failure Card

A metaphor that describes a last-attempt decision that new business owners mistakenly resort to in order to get themselves out of a tight situation but may later create negative consequences.

Glass Ceiling

A social barrier that prevents women from being promoted to managerial and executive-level positions within an organization.

Gross Profit

The profit that the company makes after deducting the costs associated with making and selling its products or the costs associated with providing its services.

Individual Operating Procedure (IOP)

When an employee was not given a Standard Operating Procedure (SOP), he or she will create their own operating procedure to get the job done.

Internal Customer

A person in an organization who needs assistance or interaction from another person to fulfill their job responsibilities.

Mission Statement

A brief description of a company's fundamental purpose that guides how the company's goals will be achieved.

Net Profit

The actual profit after working expenses not included in the calculations of gross profit have been paid.

Non-Disclosure Agreement (NDA)

A legal document that restricts the potential buyer from disclosing the financial information of his or her company.

Open-Door Policy

A communication policy in which the manager or supervisor leaves their door "open" in order to encourage openness and transparency with their employees.

Operating Loss

Occurs when a company's operating expenses exceed gross profits.

Operations Manager

An executive who leads a company's operational activities. He or she designs, executes, and manages a company's initiatives and operations.

Owner's Equity

The representation of the owner's investment in the business, minus the owner's withdrawals from the business, plus the net income (or minus net loss) since the business began.

Payroll Expense

The sum paid to employees for their labor, including employee benefits and state and federal payroll taxes.

Profitable Business Model

A company's plan that lays out product manufacturing, sales generation, fixes, and costs in an attempt to make the business profitable and viable.

Profit and Loss Statement

A statement summarizing the revenues, costs, and expenses incurred during a fiscal quarter or year.

Pro Forma Annual Budget

A predicted budget based on unusual circumstances or possible changes to the company's structure, revenues, profits, or expenses yearly.

Psychographics

The way a company's products make customers feel by studying the customer's buying habits, hobbies, spending habits, and values.

Ratio Analysis

The comparison of line items in the financial statements of a business.

Return on Total Assets (ROA)

A ratio that measures a company's earnings before interests and taxes relative to its total net assets.

Request for Proposal (RFP)

A project funding announcement posted by an organization for which companies place bids. It outlines the bidding process and contract terms and guides how the bid should be formatted.

Revenue

The income generated from normal business operations; includes discounts and deductions from returned merchandise.

Profit Margin

The amount by which revenue from sales exceeds costs in a business.

Sales Manager

A person responsible for leading and coaching a team of salespeople.

Standard Operating Procedure (SOP)

A set of step-by-step instructions compiled to help workers carry out complex routine operations.

Stranglehold

When the business owner controls every decision of the business so tightly, they do not allow for any opinions or solutions to solve the problem.

Subject Matter Expert

A person with a deep understanding of a particular process, function, technology, machine, material, or type of equipment.

.